154 STEPS
TO REVITALIZE YOUR
SUNDAY SCHOOL
AND KEEP YOUR
CHURCH GROWING

154

STEPS TO
□ REVITALIZE □
YOUR SUNDAY SCHOOL

ELMER TOWNS

VICTOR BOOKS®
A DIVISION OF SCRIPTURE PRESS PUBLICATIONS INC.
USA CANADA ENGLAND

Third printing, 1989

This book is taken from a seminar by the same name that has been taught by Dr. Towns over 200 times to over 50,000 people. The popular acceptance of the seminar gives credibility to this manuscript.

Unless otherwise noted, Scripture quotations are from *The New King James Version.* © 1979, 1980, 1982, Thomas Nelson, Inc., Publishers. Other quotes are from the *Authorized (King James) Version* (KJV).

Recommended Dewey Decimal Classification: 268
Suggested Subject Heading: SUNDAY SCHOOL; RELIGIOUS TRAINING

Library of Congress Catalog Card Number: 87-62472
ISBN: 0-89693-446-2

CONTENTS

INTRODUCTION

I love the Sunday School and appreciate its influence on my life.
I was first introduced to Sunday School when Jimmy Breland, a
Sunday School teacher, asked me if he could take me to Sunday
School. As a small boy, I faithfully attended Eastern Heights
Presbyterian Church in Savannah, Georgia, where I was
grounded in Bible content and doctrine. I was taught to bring
my offerings in a special envelope.

Because my values in life were taught to me by my mother
and reinforced in Sunday School, when I heard the Gospel
preached by a Baptist evangelist, I received Jesus Christ as my
Saviour.

Because our society is changing, some have suggested the age
of the Sunday School is past. But the future of Sunday School is
bright, and I believe God will continue to use the Sunday
School as the evangelistic and educational arm of the church.
Still, the Sunday School must adapt to continue its influence. In
my seminars, I often challenge audiences, "The Sunday School
that has been the steeple of the church must become its foundation." The Sunday School must not change its purpose but it
must go "back to the basics," for the old is again becoming new.

I believe that any church, anywhere, any time, can grow
when it is revitalized. That's because I believe in the power of

God and the influence of the Word of God. Growing a church is like growing a garden. The ground must be prepared and the seed planted properly at the correct time. The seed must be watered and be exposed to sunshine. These are principles for growing a garden, and when properly applied, new life will spring forth. There are principles for growing a Sunday School. If you apply the principles, your Sunday School will grow.

This book is based on a seminar I conduct entitled *154 Steps to Revitalize Your Sunday School and Keep Your Church Growing*. Notice I refer to 154 steps, not 154 ways. There is only one way to grow a church and that is to reach people for Jesus Christ. And there is only one way to revitalize your church, and that is through the ministry of the Holy Spirit. But there are many steps to get you there!

This book is repetitious because the book's outline follows the seminar outline. Since effective classroom teaching includes repetition, this manuscript follows the "steps" presented to live audiences. If the "steps" were changed, it would not correlate with the video and audio tapes that are available to the public.

We are living in exciting days. Churches are still growing. I began keeping records of fast-growing churches 20 years ago; and some of the fastest growth is now taking place. In 1986, the First Assembly of God in Phoenix, Arizona grew from 5,300 to over 7,500 in one year. Many of the steps used by this church are emphasized in this book.

This book will reemphasize the traditional biblical principles of evangelism and perhaps express them with new emphasis. But you will also be exposed to new techniques. Open your mind and your heart. Perhaps you can't use every suggestion, but don't close your mind to ideas just because they are new. Let this book s-t-r-e-t-c-h you to trust God (Mark 11:22-23).

I still believe that the Sunday School has a bright future and that your Sunday School can grow.

Elmer L. Towns
Lynchburg, Virginia, 1988

1

HEALTHY ATTITUDES LEAD TO SUCCESS

The Bible teaches that God's work, done in God's way, will have God's blessing. When God blesses a church or Sunday School, it will grow—both internally and externally.

But many churches are empty of people and empty of God's blessing. They are powerless to get people converted and their members are discouraged. There is no numerical growth in their ministry. The problem is a wrong attitude. When attitudes are right, other things fall into place. Note the formula for growth.

> Formula: Right attitudes + right actions = success!
> Right attitudes = right thinking about a situation or problem.
> Right actions = right acting about a situation or problem.

For a church or Sunday School to grow, it must recognize and implement: (a) correct attitudes, (b) correct objectives,

(c) correct principles, and (d) correct applications.

Sometimes churches decide they want to grow because they perceive certain benefits to the church through growth, but they are really not committed to the Word of God. This was particularly evident during the busing boom of the '70s. Hundreds of churches jumped on the busing bandwagon and purchased used buses to bring thousands of bus kids into their ministries. But some of those churches refused to make the necessary changes to their ministries to handle the influx of children. Those who got into busing with the wrong motives usually stopped running the buses very quickly when difficulties came along. They learned only after they had invested several thousands of dollars into an aborted ministry that there was a price to be paid for church growth. Note the following price that must be paid for church growth.

STEP 1 The Pastor Must Pay the Price for Growth[1]

The pastor is the leader of the church. If a church is to experience growth, the pastor must want the church to grow and be willing to pay the price. Since he is the leader of the congregation, he must be first willing to pay the price of sacrifice. Dr. Lee Roberson, who built the Sunday School of Highland Park Baptist Church in Chattanooga, Tennessee to over 11,000 in attendance, said, "Everything rises or falls on leadership." Leadership implies one is leading and people are following him. If a pastor thinks he is leading a church, but no one is following him, he is just taking a walk.

What is the price of church growth which must be paid by the pastor? First, the responsibility of growth carries the risk of failure. Just as a farmer who plants seeds in the ground fails if the plants do not come up, so the minister who sows the seed of the Word of God risks failure if nothing happens in his ministry. However, this is not just a larger head count. All church growth is not just numerical growth, though that is implied.

The second price of church growth is hard work. It is harder to pastor a growing church than a plateaued church. In many respects, pastoring is the most difficult work in the world. But

TYPES OF GROWTH
■ *Internal Growth*—when Christians or a church grows in grace and knowledge of the Lord. This is also described as nurture. ■ *External Growth*—this is numerical growth in attendance, offerings, membership, or enrollment. ■ *Biological Growth*—this is numerical growth when babies are born to church members and added to the church. ■ *Transfer Growth*—this involves Christians of "like-faith and like-practice" who join a church. Since 22 percent of Americans move to new homes each year, this means the church should target displaced Christians in their outreach program. This is not sheep-stealing but finding lost sheep. ■ *Conversion Growth*—this is numerical growth by winning lost people to Jesus Christ and bonding them to the church. ■ *Expansion Growth*—this is the growth of Christianity by planting new Sunday Schools or churches.

hard work by itself will not grow a church. A person must work smart. Technology and tools can make hard work more effective and sometimes easier.

When the pilgrims settled in the United States, they brought their tools from Europe and learned to grow corn from the Indians. Their technology was limited. They dug a hole in the ground, planted an ear of corn, and added fish for fertilizer. By working hard with his hoe, a colonist could grow the equivalent of four bushels of corn a year, or about one bushel for each month in the growing season. By the time of the Civil War,

11

farmers used mules and developed plows and other tools enabling a man to grow the equivalent of a bushel of corn a week or 16 bushels of corn a year. By the time of World War I, farmers were using tractors and other machinery. They updated their technology to save their topsoil and rotated their crops. The World War I farmer could grow a bushel of corn a day, or the equivalent of 120 bushels of corn a year. But today, with advanced technology, petrochemical fertilizer, soil analysis, and four-wheel drive tractors, a farmer can grow the equivalent of a bushel of corn for each 10 minutes of the growing season. American farmers grow more corn than the other farmers of the world because of better technology and better tools. The miracle of life in the seed has not changed; farmers can do nothing to change what God has ordered in the growth cycle. But *tools* and *technology* can improve the harvest.

Pastors can learn from the farmers. The unchanging seed is the Bible. Also, the principles of ministry have not changed. But methods have been updated! Principles never change, but methods and technology change. (A method is the application of an eternal principle to a contemporary need.) Principles are preaching, teaching, soul-winning, etc. A method might be V.B.S., bus ministry, or Sunday afternoon training union for youth. Some of these methods are not as effective as in the past. But by using the most advanced tools and technologies of the ministry, based on old-fashioned principles, we can make our hard work most effective. We can do more for God than we have ever done before.

This second cost of building a church is hard work, but never hard work alone. It will take smart work (latest tools and technologies), plus hard work.

A third cost is the pastor sharing his ministry with his members. He must learn to "give up" some things to his members so they can minister in his place. The pastor must share his ministry with his flock, for the growing church involves the ministry of the whole body to the whole body. Ministry is not limited to just the paid staff, but every person can be involved in ministry. Because every person has a spiritual gift, every "gifted" person should be using his gift (1 Cor. 7:7). A hundred years ago, only about 15 percent of our church members were involved in ministry. The remaining 85 percent were little more than spectators. But that is not the norm in growing churches today. Even though we idealistically suggest every member become involved, realistically, a growing church has 50 percent involvement.

EVERY MEMBER A MINISTER

Fourth, the pastor must recognize he has members in his church he cannot pastor, then allow others in the church to pastor them. Leadership is not doing everything, nor is it being everything. Leadership is getting the job done through other people. A wise pastor once counseled a new pastor, "Don't do the work of 10 people, put 10 people to work."

Growing churches today are led by a qualified paid staff of specialists who work together under the leadership of the senior pastor to get the job done. But that is only half the picture. A growing church must also involve a multitude of lay people who serve Jesus Christ in various forms of ministry. (See step 9 that discusses the shepherding role of laymen through Sunday School classes.)

STEP 2 The People Must Pay the Price for Church Growth
The pastor is not the only one who must be willing to pay the price of church growth. The growing church must have people who want the church to grow and are willing to pay the price. That price will involve some basic changes in their attitudes toward church life. First, they must be willing to give up that close relationship to the pastor they have in a smaller church. But because a growing church will hire staff pastors to pastor the church, they do not have to give up a close relationship to a pastor. Also, laymen will lead classes, care groups, and other

organizations where they give "pastoral care" to other laymen in the body. Even if the size of the church makes it impossible to relate socially with the senior pastor, there are others who are able to meet the needs of church members. And because these work in small groups or in specialized areas of ministry, they are probably more effective working together to meet the needs of the congregation.

Also, there are other prices to be paid by the church members. They must be willing to give up that close relationship to everyone as the church grows larger. In a large church, you can't be a close friend to everyone. Still, you will be a close friend to some. Research in this area suggests a church member knows an average of 59.7 fellow members by name regardless of the size of his church. That means in a church of 87 or 1,000, the average person is on a personal name basis with approximately 60 people. Those who selfishly try to limit a church to their circle of friends have misunderstood the meaning of a church. A church is not primarily for *koinonia* fellowship, though relationships grow out of its purpose. The Great Commission is the marching orders of the church. As the church grows, everyone will have a small Sunday School class, Bible study cell, or primary group where they will know others and be known in return. A growing church will have a multitude of these smaller fellowship groups. No one should prohibit church growth by limiting his church to those he is able to call by name.

Another price the members must pay if they want their church to grow is financial giving. Growing churches are made up of giving members, but not all churches with giving members are growing.

The members must pay the price in redirected fellowship patterns. The growing church is not a crowd, but an army. It is comparatively easy to get a crowd of people to come to hear an entertaining quartet sing or for a sacred music concert. But a concert on Sunday morning is not a church, even if it is followed by a Gospel message. A church involves people teaching, giving, and serving on committees where decisions are made about the church. The church is not a church when it is just people who come to hear a sermon. A church is the body of gifted believers edifying itself (Eph. 4:11-16). As the church grows larger, everyone must redirect his fellowship relationships.

The church must open leadership circles. This is a price of growth. I get excited about the numbers in large churches, but numbers alone never are the cause. I get excited about the growing number of laymen who are involved in ministry. The lay ministry is a sleeping bear that has awakened in American churches and will have a larger influence in the future.

STEP 3   The Goal Is the Great Commission

The growing church must agree on its corporate goal which is found in the Great Commission. "Go ye therefore, and *teach* all nations, *baptizing* them in the name of the Father, and of the Son, and of the Holy Ghost: *Teaching* them to observe all things whatsoever I have commanded you: and, lo, I am with you always, even unto the end of the world" (Matt. 28:19-20, KJV, italics added).

Notice the three emphasized words which are key to the strategy of the Great Commission, a strategy which results in numerical church growth. The first word, teach, is translated from the Greek word *matheteuo* which literally means "make disciples." Disciple-making is more than evangelism at the county fair, which means to get people to make a decision for Christ. We must get people to make decisions to become disciples of Jesus Christ, but we must do more than involve them in a decision. A disciple is a follower: the new convert follows Christ in confession, baptism, godliness, tithing, and service. The lost person must make a decision to follow Christ, then follow Christ to the church for public confession in baptism, follow Christ in service, and follow Christ in holiness.

The second key strategy word is baptizing. The old word for baptizing was "churching." A convert should be committed to Christ and His church. Bonding is a key thought in church growth. Bonding has the result of "super glue" as opposed to the frailty of paste or mucilage. We need to bond new believers to our churches so that those we reach with the Gospel become assimilated into a growing church.

The third word in our strategy is also translated teaching, but is a different Greek word than the previous one for teaching. The verb here is *didaskontes*, meaning teaching in the sense of giving instruction. Those who become disciples of Christ must become a part of His church and be taught His commands if they are to grow spiritually and become a part of a growing church. And teaching is where Sunday School becomes an indispensable foundation of church growth.

2

RECOGNIZE THE NATURE OF THE SUNDAY SCHOOL

Some people have the wrong idea about Sunday School and as a result fail to see its importance in the revitalization and growth of their church. They think Sunday School is only for kids, or is an out-dated method. Others think of Sunday School as a contest that rewards losers with a pie in the face. Someone repeating this tortured view said, "When is a school not a school? When it is a Sunday School!"

Just as the New Testament church was built on teaching and preaching, so the modern biblical church must be built on Bible study in Sunday School and exhortation in the preaching service. Sunday School is functionally defined as the reaching, teaching, winning, maturing arm of the church. This fourfold nature of Sunday School is perhaps best expressed in an Old Testament verse which has often been used in the historic Sunday School conventions to express the nature of Sunday School. "Gather the people together, men and women and little ones, and the stranger who is within your gates, that they may hear and that they may learn to fear the Lord your God, and carefully observe all the words of this law" (Deut. 31:12). This verse reflects the four distinct areas of Sunday School ministry.

STEP 4   Sunday School Is the Reaching Arm

First, Sunday School is the evangelistic reaching arm of the church. Reaching is defined as making contact with a person and motivating him to give an honest hearing to the Gospel. Since evangelism is giving out the Gospel, reaching is basically pre-evangelism, for it is what we do to get people to listen to the Gospel. In our text, it is expressed in the word "gather." Note those who are gathered, (1) fathers, (2) mothers, (3) little ones or children, and (4) "the stranger." Most church members have someone within their sphere of influence who is a stranger to the church who could be gathered into the church.

STEP 5   Sunday School Is the Teaching Arm

Second, Sunday School is the teaching arm of the church. Teaching is guiding the learning activities that meet human needs. The first step of teaching is expressed in the words of the verse, "that they may hear." The ultimate step of teaching is "that they may learn."

STEP 6   Sunday School Is the Winning Arm

Sunday School is also the arm of the church that wins people to Christ. Winning is defined as communicating the Gospel in an understandable manner and motivating a person to respond. The Old Testament expression "fear the Lord" meant bringing a person to reverential trust. It was a concept of salvation. Today we might describe "fear the Lord" as a person getting saved, receiving Christ, or trusting the Lord for salvation.

STEP 7   Sunday School Is the Maturing Arm

Finally, Sunday School is the maturing arm of the church. Maturing is bringing a person to completion or making him well-rounded. One of the objectives of every Sunday School should be the maturing of its members so that they "carefully observe all the words of this law." Some call this nurturing, others call it training.

This is our definition: the Sunday School is the reaching, teaching, winning, maturing arm of the church. However, this definition becomes a mosaic when applied to individual churches. Just as it takes all the pieces of tile to make up a mosaic picture, so it takes all four aspects of the definition to describe a beautiful Sunday School. But some destroy the beauty when they focus on one section of the tile and lose the whole picture. This happens when some have a strong *reaching* dynamic, so that there are an abundance of visitors, such as a Sunday School with a dominant busing outreach. These focus on numbers so that they lose the total perspective. Some are strong *teaching* Sunday Schools, with a deep commitment to Bible mastery. Other Sunday Schools are committed to soul-winning and their success is measured by how many they have won to Christ or prepared for church membership. Finally, some Sunday Schools are maturity oriented. These are committed to teaching environment and relationships. They measure their effectiveness by the quality of change in the lifestyles of their pupils.

From generation to generation there seems to be a different emphasis on the character of Sunday School. In the early '70s the emphasis was on reaching with attention given to Sunday School busing and Sunday School contests. The current emphasis is on the teaching arm. The Sunday School was the steeple, but is becoming the foundation. The steeple is the most visible part of a church building and its most symbolic emblem. The teaching foundation of the Sunday School will give the church of the twenty-first century stability and direction. In keeping with this shift in emphasis is an obvious attendance pattern. Visitors attend the preaching service first, not like past years where they visited Sunday School first. The average American Sunday School runs 24 percent under the attendance of the average church service.

3

RECOGNIZE THE ROLE OF THE SUNDAY SCHOOL TEACHER

Sunday School teaching is one of the greatest opportunities in the world to serve God. But with that opportunity comes responsibility. Teaching Sunday School is different from most teaching. It involves a supernatural curriculum, the Bible; it involves a supernatural command, the Great Commission; it involves a supernatural unction and enduement, God's call and bestowal of gifts; it involves the supernatural power, the enlightenment of the Holy Spirit. Therefore, the teacher who teaches in Sunday School should be more than an instructor who is using the Bible as content. A Sunday School teacher has the responsibility for the spiritual welfare of his students.

STEP 8 A Teacher Is More than an Instructor
A Sunday School teacher is not just an instructor, like a saved public school teacher who is teaching the Bible. A Sunday School teacher has a much broader task than just communicating biblical truth.

Many have difficulty recruiting teachers for their Sunday Schools. Perhaps it is because they are looking for the wrong thing. Begin the process of recruiting a teacher by giving a spiritual gift inventory. This is not a test to determine failure or passing, but rather a reflection of what spiritual gifts a person possesses. Then, do not try to talk people into teaching Sunday School who do not have the gift of teaching. The Church Growth Institute, Lynchburg, Virginia has a spiritual gift inventory that identifies two expressions of the spiritual gift of teaching. The first is the gift of teaching where the person has a desire to study, to discover new truth, then communicate it in the instructing process. This is not the gift that best describes the Sunday School teacher, though many Sunday School teachers have this gift. The second gift is the "pastor-teacher" described in Ephesians 4:11, "And He Himself gave . . . some pastors and teachers." The pastor-teacher uses instruction to nurture his pupils. Even though the *King James Version* separates the two words, "pastors, and teachers," the Greek language joins them as one function. The pastor is a teacher. That brings us to the next step. The Sunday School teacher is a shepherd.

STEP 9   *A Teacher Shepherds a Class*
A Sunday School teacher is a shepherd. A woman who has four small children around a table in a church basement should be doing a lot more than telling Bible stories about baby Moses in the bulrushes, or Noah's ark. She should be giving spiritual care to her pupils, which involves telling Bible stories. Just as a pastor shepherds his flock in more ways than preaching, so a Sunday School teacher cares for the Sunday School flock in more ways than teaching.

Everything the pastor is to his flock, the teacher is to his Sunday School class. The same Greek word is used for pastor and shepherd, suggesting their work is similar.

WORK OF A SHEPHERD
1 Leads the Flock.
2 Feeds the Flock.
3 Protects the Flock.

STEP 10 A Teacher Is the Pastor's Extension

The Sunday School teacher is the extension of pastoral ministry into the life of the class. Just as an extension helps you get to hard-to-reach places, so a Sunday School teacher helps the pastor reach hard-to-reach people (at least hard for him to reach). A pastor can't always reach down to a three-year-old boy, but a Sunday School teacher can. Classes need to be more than content centers, they need to be shepherding centers.

The Apostle Paul's advice to the pastors of the church at Ephesus is also a challenge to Sunday School teachers today. "Therefore take heed to yourselves and to all the flock, among which the Holy Spirit has made you *overseers*, to *shepherd* the church of God, which He purchased with His own blood. For I know this, that after my departure savage wolves will come in among you, not sparing the flock. . . . Therefore *watch*" (Acts 20:28-31, italics added). Notice the three words that are emphasized in these verses. These words contain the threefold job description of a pastor or Sunday School teacher. First, he is to oversee the flock, which is leading sheep. Second, he shepherds or feeds the flock, which is giving instruction. Third, he protects the flock by watching over them.

STEP 11 A Teacher Is a Leader

How does the Sunday School teacher "shepherd" the flock in his care? He does so by fulfilling the three primary functions of the shepherd. First, a shepherd leads the flock. The greatest influence of many Sunday School teachers has been the result of their leading by example.

STEP 12 A Teacher Is a Feeder

Second, a shepherd feeds the flock. While good Bible teaching will not guarantee your class will grow, poor teaching will hinder its growth.

STEP 13 A Teacher Is a Protector

Finally, a shepherd protects the flock. Jesus told Peter to "tend My sheep" (John 21:16). A Sunday School teacher visits the students who are absent to protect them from backsliding.

One of the best known and loved passages in all Scripture is the Twenty-third Psalm. In this passage, David describes the care he received at the hand of his Shepherd, the Lord. The example of the Lord who is our Shepherd is a constant challenge to the Sunday School teacher who is trying to be to his class what the Lord is to him.

STEP 14 The Superintendent Uses the Gift of Administration

If the Sunday School teacher is an extension of the pastoral ministry into the life of the class, then the Sunday School superintendent is the extension of the pastor's organizational and administrative responsibilities, supervising the educational program of the church. Someone in the Sunday School needs to have a passion for organization. That person is the Sunday School superintendent. While the teacher and superintendent have different responsibilities in the function of a growing Sunday School, when each performs his duties faithfully, both free the pastor to devote his energies into his primary area of ministry.

The Sunday School superintendent may have different titles in different places such as Coordinator or Supervisor; and in some churches the Director or Minister of Christian Education functions as the superintendent.

The Sunday School superintendent is usually responsible to a Board or Committee of Christian Education that determines the (1) job description, (2) budget, (3) policy, and (4) curriculum selection. Of course, the superintendent gives insight, counsel, and direction to the Board of Christian Education. In some churches there is no Board or Committee of Christian Education and the superintendent is directly accountable to the pastor who gives direction to the position.

The Sunday School superintendent is basically the manager of the Sunday School. Managers are not owners, chairmen, or the final seat of authority. Managers carry out their tasks for another person, or group of people. A manager has responsibility to manage in four areas: (1) people (personnel manager), (2) money (budget manager), (3) time (schedule manager), and (4) resources (building and equipment manager).

Just because a person has been an outstanding teacher does not necessarily make him qualified to be promoted to the position of superintendent. Administer a spiritual gift inventory to determine those who have the spiritual gift of "helps" or "administration." In addition, the superintendent should have experience working in the Sunday School to give background and experience for the decisions he must make.

Good management is essential for growth. However, some mistakenly think that a well-managed Sunday School is the cause that brings about the growth effect. Not so. You can't grow a Sunday School with good management alone, but you can't grow a Sunday School without it.

STEP 15 Barriers Prohibit Growth

Why is it that some churches just don't grow? Part of the answer to that question is found in recognizing the barriers to evangelism. According to Donald McGavran, "People like to become Christians without crossing racial, linguistic, or class barriers."

McGavran's statement is not a normative statement but rather a descriptive statement. This is not the way it should be, rather, it is the way it is. God made man a social creature, and barriers that interfere with social relationships may have a profound spiritual influence on him. The more barriers that are placed between a person and Christ, the more difficult it is to win him to Christ. If our churches are going to grow, we need to remove as many barriers as possible to make it easier for people to become Christians.

BARRIERS
E-0 Spiritual Barriers
E-1 Stained-Glass Barriers
E-2 Cultural and Class Barriers
E-3 Language Barriers

Of course there will be some barriers which can never be removed, i.e., the offense of the Cross. Some will never be saved because the message of the Cross, which is an intricate part of the Gospel, is offensive to them. Grace is also a barrier to some for they want to do good works to be saved and resist being saved by grace alone (Eph. 2:8-9). We cannot remove these primary barriers. The barriers we can remove are secondary and are not related directly to the root of Christianity.

The E-1 Barrier has been called "the stained-glass barrier." Church growth writers speak of E-1 Evangelism which is evangelism that overcomes the barrier that relates to the church building. "Stained glass" reflects more than windows or church sanctuaries. It is a symbolic word for those things that stand between those on the outside of the church and getting them inside to hear the Gospel. These barriers make it difficult for a person to attend a Sunday School or church service or continue to attend. The stained-glass barrier includes such things as poor location, inadequate parking, and unkept or poorly maintained facilities.

When the parking lot is full, it is a barrier for the visitor to find a parking place in the street. Some think that adequate parking or eliminating other barriers will cause church growth. No! There must be a dynamic that draws people to Jesus Christ. The church must have warm services and the pastor must preach with power. A barrier just makes it harder to reach people; it does not make it impossible to reach people. Eliminating barriers makes it easier to reach people.

Stained-glass barriers also include perceptions, such as a lost person's dislike for a denomination's name or what an unchurched person remembers about a particular church. Some have had a bad experience with a church member from a certain denomination, hence the church name is a barrier. A church split becomes a barrier to the neighborhood, making it harder for both halves to reach people for Christ.

The E-2 Barrier is a cultural and class barrier. It hinders the evangelistic outreach of some churches. This principle recognizes members of certain cultures who may not wish to attend a church which is predominantly made up of members of another culture. It is not a matter of liking the people of another culture or class, it is being comfortable with their different values. While the church must be the church of the open door willing to admit all, normally, members of a culture different from the members of the church will have difficulty becoming assimilated into the social life of the congregation.

At a meeting of the Evangelical Theological Society in Los Angeles, a pioneering church planter to West Los Angeles (Hispanic) explained cross-cultural ministry to a group of Anglo evangelical theologians. He explained that when Anglos tried to pioneer a church in his community, he knew they would probably fail when he saw them roll a piano into the new church.

"A piano is an Anglo musical instrument, not a Mexican one," he explained. Further he noted, "What reaches the heart of a Mexican, doesn't always work with Anglos. There are few pianos in Mexico. A guitar plays on the heart of Mexicans, and a young man woos a young girl with a guitar because it is heart music.

"If you want to reach the heart of Mexicans with the Gospel, use the guitar, not the piano," he concluded.

Related to cultural barriers are also class barriers. The difference among classes is not primarily money but rather the values that surround their background. Music expresses the heart worship to God. Just as music divides the cultures, so it expresses the different values of different classes. Just as members of the lower classes do not usually like the "long-hair" music of the classics, so upper classes often fail to appreciate the twang of "Country and Western" even when the words are biblical. Never make the mistake of concluding that the music enjoyed by the "lower class" is inferior to music enjoyed by the "upper class." Music affirms the soul and is the person's way of magnifying God. Since "the Father is seeking such to worship Him" (John 4:23), then God enjoys the "Nashville" type Gospel music of a hillbilly church, just as much as He enjoys the anthems from a church with a full pipe organ—if the music comes from the heart of the worshiper.

Linguistic barriers are perhaps the most obvious barriers to evangelism. E-3 Evangelism is that which overcomes language barriers. People like to hear God in their heart language (the language in which they think) even when they themselves speak a second language. Al Henson began the Lighthouse Baptist Church in Nashville, Tennessee intent on reaching greater Nashville with the Gospel. When he learned many Laotians were moving to his city, he sent his people out into the streets to reach them with the Gospel. Soon the church had a preaching service which about 200 Laotians were attending. They worshiped in the Laotian language and a layman preached to them in English as a Laotian translated the Gospel into their mother tongue. When they learned English, Henson canceled the Laotian service and brought them into his English service. But only about 50 made the transition. When Henson realized the problem, he began the Laotian service again. The church was able to continue reaching Laotians with the Gospel. The pastor learned that even though the Laotians could speak English, they preferred to hear God speak their "heart language."

My church, Thomas Road Baptist Church in Lynchburg, Virginia, has a Friday evening service in the Korean language for the area residents not fluent in English. They sing, pray, and preach in Korean. They are even baptized in Korean.

The first step in overcoming barriers is to identify those of different cultures, classes, and languages. The Christian leader has the responsibility to make the first step. Paul said, "I have become all things to all men, that I might by all means save some" (1 Cor. 9:22).

In the treatment of any physical sickness, the first step is always diagnosis. This process may require days and even weeks of testing, but it is essential to proper treatment. Viruses are treated differently than bacteria, and even among viruses, one particular drug may be more effective than another. So it is with the barriers to evangelism. It is needful to identify the classification of the barrier (E-0, E-1, E-2, or E-3).

Remember, people are all different, and the barriers standing in the way of each are different. The key is to identify the

27

specific barrier and tear it down. If it is one the prospect has erected in his own mind, you have to take the initiative and cross the barrier. If the barrier is in your church, again you must take the initiative to change it.

You may not have erected the barrier, but you must remove it. Do not let your fears keep you from being a witness. The task begins with gaining victory over fears. While the world, the flesh, and the devil are the enemies, they are not to be feared. Jesus prayed that believers (John 17:5-26) should not be taken out of the world but that they should be insulated against it. His petition was "that You should keep them from the evil one" (v. 15). Victory is available to the believer by his walking in the Spirit rather than in the flesh. "Yet in all these things we are more than conquerors through Him who loved us" (Rom. 8:37). For the believer, the key to victory over fear is faith in God and His promises.

Once Christians have overcome their own fears, they are free to begin tearing away the fears of the unsaved. This is done by establishing redemptive friendships. This exposes them to Christians, the Christian lifestyle, and the joys of the Christian life. In Luke 14:12-13, Jesus suggested that when believers give a dinner they should not invite only friends and relatives, because they will only feel obligated to return your hospitality. Instead, he said, invite the poor, maimed, lame, and blind. (This means those who are rejected by others.) When they begin to see that Christians are people much like themselves, the stained-glass barrier begins to dissolve.

We must not be judgmental. Christ alone is the righteous Judge, and Paul indicated that He will judge His own servants (1 Cor. 4). Our task is to accept the unsaved man as he is, win him to ourselves, so that we can lead him to a saving knowledge of Jesus Christ. Once he has become a new creation in Christ (2 Cor. 5:17), the Holy Spirit will work through the Word of God to bring about the needed changes in his conduct and lifestyle.

4

RECOGNIZING WHY SUNDAY SCHOOLS ARE NOT GROWING

STEP 16   A Healthy Church Body Will Grow

The church must be healthy if it is going to grow. The best biblical analogy to represent the church is the body, and a physical body will grow when it is healthy, fed, and exercised. A body does not need to be challenged, coaxed, or have a goal to grow. The body automatically grows when it is healthy. When a local church body is healthy, it will grow internally and externally. Perhaps your church is not growing, or your Sunday School is in trouble. Are you properly feeding it the Word of God? Are you properly exercising it in prayer and witnessing? If you think your church is healthy, but it is not growing, perhaps it has a disease. When the body has a disease, it does not grow in a healthy manner.

In medical school, pathology is one of the first courses studied by future doctors. Pathology is the study of disease. A doctor cannot treat a sickness until he understands its causes. He must know what makes a person sick before he can suggest a remedy or prescription. Even then, the doctor does not make a person well; the body has the energy to heal itself and grow itself. So it is with the body of Christ. When a church is sick, no leader can make it well. When he removes the cause of the

29

illness, the body heals itself.

This section examines the diseases that prohibit a church from growing. When we know and remove the causes of church diseases, the body will heal itself.

STEP 17   Cure Ethnikitis by Opening to All

The first disease is called "ethnikitis." It is the inbred allegiance of the church to one ethnic group and its lack of adaptation or openness to other groups. This disease occurs when communities change their ethnic character and churches fail to adapt to those changes. Sometimes a symptom of ethnikitis is what has been called "White Flight," where the traditional WASP (White Anglo-Saxon Protestant) churches move out of their traditional communities as the ethnic character of the area changes.

In our growing nation, our churches must be multi-ethnic, reaching to every new family or group of people moving into our neighborhoods. In one sense, the small neighborhood church is a homogeneous unit, yet the growing church must be a heterogeneous unit (the open door to all people), yet made up of homogeneous cells (classes and cells that will attract and minister to each group within its neighborhood).

HOW TO SOLVE ETHNIKITIS
1 Begin Bible classes or cells for new groups.
2 Hire staff members who represent the new groups moving into the neighborhood.
3 Begin a second-language preaching service.
4 If the church moves to another neighborhood, dedicate the building to spawn a continuing church.
5 New groups do not automatically visit existing churches, they must be aggressively sought and brought into the church fellowship.

The church that suffers ethnikitis is first, sinning against God, second, disobeying the Great Commission, and third, allowing a cancer to fester within its body.

STEP 18   Cure Old Age by Reaching People In Transition

Old age is another disease of church growth. This disease describes the community more than the church. When a church and the community become "old" so that not many people are moving in or out of the neighborhood, it is described as suffering "old age." Though there are many advantages of a stable community, there are some disadvantages. When no one is moving in, there are no prospects for evangelism, nor are there unchurched who are candidates for church membership, hence no numerical growth.

Churches are candidates for growth when they are located in growing areas such as in new housing subdivisions, or areas where the population is mobile. This is because when people move they go through a transition in their lives which St. Augustine referred to as "the seasons of the soul." This means people are ripe for evangelism, like fruit for the harvest. During times when people move, they go through culture shock or disequilibrium. The uncertainty created by culture shock creates a void in a person's life. This emptiness drives him to find satisfaction, and since the greatest satisfaction is Christ, the person is a candidate for salvation.

Dr. Thomas Holmes, professor of psychiatry at the University of Washington School of Medicine in Seattle, Washington, devoted 25 years of research to the subject of stress-producing experiences in life and rated the 43 most common crisis experiences. The more severe the crisis, the more likely one is entering a season of the soul.

It is difficult to build a growing Sunday School in a stagnant neighborhood. When everyone is stable and no one is moving geographically, they are also probably not moving spiritually. And when people move out of a neighborhood (such as a dying mining town or a small farming town), it is difficult to see growth.

THE SEASONS OF THE SOUL*	

Rank	Crisis	Points
1	Death of a spouse	100
2	Divorce	73
3	Marital separation	65
4	Jail term	63
5	Death of close family member	63
6	Personal injury or illness	53
7	Marriage	50
8	Job firing	47
9	Marital reconciliation	45
10	Retirement	45
11	Change in health of family member	44
12	Pregnancy	44
13	Sexual difficulties	39
14	Gain of new family member	39
15	Business readjustment	39
16	Change in financial state	38
17	Death of a close friend	37
18	Change to different line of work	36
19	Change in number of arguments with spouse	35
20	Mortgage more than $10,000	31
21	Foreclosure of mortgage or loan	30
22	Change in responsibilities at work	29
23	Departure of son or daughter from home	29
24	Trouble with in-laws	29
25	Outstanding personal achievement	28
26	Wife's beginning or stopping work	26
27	Beginning or end of school	26
28	Change in living conditions	25
29	Change of personal habits	24
30	Trouble with boss	23
31	Change in work hours or conditions	20
32	Change in residence	20
33	Change in schools	20
34	Change in recreation	19
35	Change in church activities	19
36	Change in social activities	18
37	Mortgage or loan less than $10,000	17
38	Change in sleeping habits	16
39	Change in number of family gatherings	15
40	Change in eating habits	15
41	Vacation	13
42	Christmas	12
43	Minor violations of the law	11

*Source: Tim LaHaye, *How to Win over Depression* (New York: Bantam Books, 1976), pp. 99-100.

Years ago it was observed the Sunday School bus ministry was more effective in trailer courts, housing projects, or the poor areas of town (the poorer economically a family, the more often they are likely to move their residences, hence they are candidates for the Gospel). This discussion of the seasons of the soul does not take away from the supernatural nature of conversion. However, God can use natural causes (the death of a loved one) to motivate a person to seek salvation. Then God regenerates that person and gives him eternal life.

HOW TO OVERCOME OLD AGE
1 Reach people going through transitions (the seasons of the soul) in the hospital ministry, weddings, funerals, birth of a baby, etc. **2** Don't set unrealistic growth goals. **3** Give attention to maintenance ministry, not growth ministry. **4** Begin pioneer works in another community that has growth.

STEP 19 Cure People Blindness by Becoming Need Conscious

A third disease of the church which can hinder growth is called "people blindness." This refers to the inability of the church to see the spiritual, social, and community needs. The key to an effective, growing ministry may be summarized in the expression "find a hurt and heal it." Hence, a church must have a "vision" of needs, then develop a program to meet the needs of people and the community. A church with a food service for the poor will attract and minister to the poor. Some churches have ministries for the hearing impaired (sign language interpreting), classes for the mentally retarded, single parent families, widowed, or newly married. The church that is sensitive to the aches and pains of its body will always have a ministry.

A 59-year-old widow moved to Burlington, North Carolina,

but just didn't seem to fit into the churches she visited. When her son visited to find out the problem, he phoned a dozen churches before he found one that had a class for widows. When she joined the church it didn't just add 1 to the roll. A daughter and her family of 4 came into the church. Then a sister-in-law and her family of 3 joined the church. A church that was sensitive to widows added 10 to its roll, not just 1.

HOW TO SOLVE PEOPLE BLINDNESS

1 Create a task force of members to brainstorm the potential community needs not being met by the church.

2 Have the task force brainstorm possible programs to meet these needs.

3 Study the "philosophy of ministry" in churches similar to yours that minister in neighborhoods similar to yours.

4 Plan special Sunday School classes or Bible studies for "need" groups.

5 Have the pastor preach on the definition of ministry, "communicating the Gospel to people at their point of need."

STEP 20 Cure Koinonitis by Focusing on Outreach

"Koinonitis" is the next disease that hinders church growth. This word is based on the Greek stem *koin* which is the root of the "fellowship" words in the New Testament. *Koinonia* is fellowship. But it is possible for a church to go to "seed" on fellowship. When relationship among members is so important that outreach is neglected, that church has a disease—koinonitis. Technically, koinonitis is inbred allegiance or fellowship with itself and that becomes its unique commitment. The Great Commission is the aim of the church but some groups have made other things their top priority. When secondary things (internal fellowship) become the primary test of Christianity, the church

34

will have difficulty maintaining sustained growth.

HOW TO SOLVE KOINONITIS
1 Organize a Friend Day so that everyone is accountable to enroll a friend for attendance on a special day.
2 Give everyone in the church a spiritual gift inventory so that those with the gift of evangelism can be identified and involved in a weekly outreach program.
3 Create new Bible study groups or adult Sunday School classes that will put new members and old members on an equal basis, hence making it possible to bond new members to the church.
4 The pastor must create an "outreach attitude" from the pulpit that focuses the initiative of the congregation on the unchurched.
5 Create a follow-up program to bond visitors to the church (see steps 60-76).

STEP 21   Cure Sociological Strangulation by Adding Space
A fifth disease hindering church growth has been called "sociological strangulation." This refers to the situation where the facilities (church sanctuary and classrooms) are not capable of providing for growth. Just as you can't pour 12 ounces of milk into a 6-ounce glass without spilling it, so you can't get 200 people in a church that is designed for 100 people. They will spill. And like spilt milk that is lost, some people visit the overcrowded church and never return. Then we cry over spilt milk.

As a general rule of thumb, when the pews are 80 percent full, the church will not grow. Churches are like a box of corn flakes; you never get a full box, you have to allow for settlement. This rule cannot be reversed. Space will not make a church grow, but lack of space will keep it from growing. There

must be a dynamic outreach of the Gospel to produce growth.
Sociological strangulation also applies to the parking lot. In
our day of convenience-market mentality and fast-food frenzy,
people will not go where there is no place for them to park, and
this applies to the church. There is a correlation between the
number of parking spaces and the church growth.

How much can your church grow in its present facilities?
Have the head usher count "empty seats" during the worship
service to get an accurate picture of how much growth can be
expected in the present auditorium. Then have an usher count
the number of spaces in the parking lot to determine the growth
potential. Do not plan for growth that is larger than the empty
space in the auditorium and parking lot.

When you do not have space, plan a second church service,
then a second Sunday School. David Rhodenheizzer, pastor of
Calvary Road Baptist Church, Alexandria, Virginia, motivated
the church upward to 400 in attendance during 1983, but
reached an upper plateau. I told him he needed to begin a
second preaching service. At first he was reluctant, but shortly
after going to two services, attendance reached 750. I told him
he would need a third service to reach 1,000. Again he resisted,
but in 1985 the church reached over 1,000 when they estab-

SOLVING SOCIOLOGICAL STRANGULATION
1 Begin a second worship service.
2 Move adult Sunday School classes off the church campus to local restaurants, banquet rooms at a hotel/motel, homes, or rooms provided for public service.
3 Begin a Youth Worship Service to give more room for adults. (This is going to two worship services.)
4 Make long-range plans to construct new facilities.
5 Bring in a consultant to guide the church in solving the space problem.

lished three worship services. Again remember, extra worship services will not produce church growth, they only allow the church that is dynamic to grow. The law of sociological strangulation suggests that lack of space will keep a church from outreach and growth.

STEP 22 Cure Arrested Spiritual Growth by Prioritizing Ministry

A sixth church growth disease has been called "arrested spiritual development." When a church stops growing internally, it ultimately stops growing externally. Things that arrest spiritual development include lack of prayer, sin, lack of Bible, and no vision. Internal growth (growth in grace) becomes the foundation of numerical growth.

HEALING ARRESTED SPIRITUAL GROWTH
1 Conduct a stewardship campaign to teach church members biblical stewardship of time, talents, and treasure.
2 Pastors should address known cases of unconfessed sin among members personally and (if necessary) publicly.
3 Organize the church to pray for the resolution of church problems and needs of the community.
4 Conduct a Friend Day campaign to motivate church members to reach out beyond themselves to the lost in their sphere of influence.
5 Institute new times/meetings for prayer and intercession. If the traditional prayer meeting has lost its vitality, perhaps a series of early morning prayer meetings before members go to their employment will revitalize the church.

STEP 23   Cure St. John's Syndrome by . . .
Returning to Original Purpose

The seventh church growth disease is the "St. John syndrome." This condition occurs during a transition from the first generation who began the church with a pioneering spirit to the second generation which tends to be content to settle down. First generation members are usually pioneers who want to expand the church, but second generation church members are usually settlers who want to settle down on the land.

The term St. John is named for John who wrote the Book of Revelation that describes the church at Ephesus that left its first love (Rev. 2:4). When a church leaves its love for Christ as expressed in soul-winning and teaching the Word of God, it has St. John's syndrome.

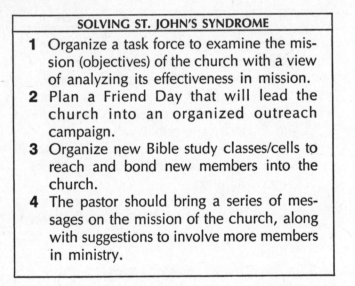

SOLVING ST. JOHN'S SYNDROME
1 Organize a task force to examine the mission (objectives) of the church with a view of analyzing its effectiveness in mission.
2 Plan a Friend Day that will lead the church into an organized outreach campaign.
3 Organize new Bible study classes/cells to reach and bond new members into the church.
4 The pastor should bring a series of messages on the mission of the church, along with suggestions to involve more members in ministry.

STEP 24   Cure Senility by Organizing a Strategy

Sometimes a body will develop diseases when a person does not properly attend to himself. When a body is not fed properly or is not kept clean, it will eventually develop a disease or become sick.

Senility in church growth occurs because of an absence of strategy for growth and revitalization. A church will not grow unless it has a workable strategy that gives direction for all of its energies. Some churches may want to grow, but do not experience growth because they do not know how to grow.

SCORE YOUR CHURCH		
	Serious Problem	No Problem
ETHNIKITIS		
OLD AGE		
PEOPLE BLINDNESS		
KOINONITIS		
SOCIOLOGICAL STRANGULATION		
ARRESTED SPIRITUAL DEVELOPMENT		
ST. JOHN'S SYNDROME		
SENILITY		

5

RETURN TO TRADITIONAL LAWS OF SUNDAY SCHOOL GROWTH

Building a church or Sunday School is not the same as attracting a crowd. Some churches are similar to a Gospel concert or a Bible conference. These churches attract a crowd by their music or their speaker. But a New Testament church is more than an assembly of people who gather on Sunday morning. A church is like an army that must be recruited, trained, deployed, and led into battle.

During the early '70s there were many large churches that attracted a crowd primarily by bus ministry or through advertisement. Many of these churches are a shell of their former size some 10 years later. Why? Because they never got their converts into Sunday School classes where they were taught the Word of God. They never trained their laymen for ministry. They were not New Testament churches in the full meaning of the word.

One of the trends in Sunday School today is expressed in the statement, "The Sunday School that has been the steeple of the church must become the foundation." The steeple is the attracting symbol of the church. The previously strong evangelistic arm of Sunday School which in the past attracted people to the church through campaigns, busing, etc., must be replaced by a strong teaching arm of the truth. Then the Sunday School has a foundation to reach out to the lost and keep them when it reaches them.

Developing a strategy to build a church is similar to developing a strategy to build a pyramid. To lift attendance high, you must broaden the base. Like any pyramid, the higher the pyramid, the broader the base. If Sunday School has become the foundation of the church, the church will grow only as that base is broadened. Growing churches today are returning to the traditional laws of Sunday School growth and implementing these principles into their ministry.

The traditional laws of Sunday School growth were developed by an unlikely preacher who astounded his fellow pastors by building a large church. This young minister began his ministry by building an east Texas church from an average of approximately 50 or 60 to over 1,000 in attendance. People questioned how he did it, especially in light of the fact it was common knowledge he was not a great pulpiteer. It was assumed great churches were built through great preaching. Because of his success in church building, the pastor was invited to address a convention for pastors.

He challenged his fellow pastors to build Sunday Schools as the foundation for building churches. He said, "If you build your Sunday Schools, they will build your churches." Rather than preach a traditional sermon, he shared with them the laws of Sunday School growth that had helped him build his church. He challenged them with a motto, "From 52 to 1 by 52." In 1927, the Southern Baptist Convention was the fifty-second largest denomination in America. He urged them to a 25-year plan of action that would make them the largest denomination by 1952. Though the motto was never formally adopted, the Southern Baptist Convention took the message to heart and used the laws of Sunday School growth to build great churches and Sunday Schools.

STEP 25   The Law of the Teacher
The first of these laws declared there must be 1 Sunday School worker/teacher for every 10 pupils. (Authorities are not agreed

whether this means only the teacher, or all support staff.) This percentage of 1 to 10 did not have to apply to every class but reflected an overall Sunday School average. Younger children need more workers, hence their classes are usually smaller with 1 worker for every 4 or 5 pupils. Fewer workers are necessary in adult classes, hence they can become larger with 12 or 15 pupils in a class. Still, the key is laborers. When Jesus went through the towns and villages, He saw the multitudes and was moved with compassion for them. Then Jesus urged His disciples, "Pray ye therefore the Lord of the harvest, that He will send forth laborers into His harvest" (Matt. 9:38, KJV). Sunday School growth begins with the law of the teacher. To increase your Sunday School by 50 in the next few months, begin with a recruitment campaign to enlist 5 new teachers.

STEP 26   The Law of the Class
A second law of Sunday School growth is the law of teaching units. This law stated there should be one teaching center for every 10 pupils. This does not mean one classroom because in some rooms there are three or more teaching centers, especially among the smaller children's departments that use the activity teaching centers. Again, the law of teaching units is a general statement that applies to the total Sunday School. Some adult classes will have 15 or 25 pupils, while children's classes will have 4 or 5 pupils.

STEP 27   Organize Classes into Departments
As your Sunday School grows, organize classes into departments averaging about 40 pupils. Again, every department will not have 40 pupils, as this is a Sunday-School-wide average. Adult departments are larger and children's departments are smaller. This is an important law which explains one of the danger levels or plateaus of Sunday School growth.

STEP 28   The Law of Administration
Administration of a growing Sunday School is imperative. As the Sunday School grows in numbers, administrators must be

added to give supervision for efficiency and continual outreach. This fourth law recommends that administrators represent 5 percent of the total attendance. The administrators are the grease and the oil that keep the Sunday School machinery lubricated. Since the church is both an organism and organization, the Sunday School must have organization to keep the spiritual outreach from breaking down.

What is organization? It is putting the right person in the right place, to do the right thing in the right way, with the right tools, at the right time, for the right purpose.

DUTIES OF THE SUNDAY SCHOOL SUPERINTENDENT

1 To provide counsel and guidance to his teachers as they plan class events.
2 To enthusiastically promote the total Sunday School program and special promotions.
3 To coordinate the various activities of different classes and departments.
4 To provide leadership and direction to the Sunday School.
5 To recruit and train teachers and workers for the Sunday School.
6 To shepherd his flock, those teachers and workers who are under his authority.

STEP 29   The Law of the Classroom

There must be educational space for growth. This law of Sunday School growth was implied earlier with the problem of sociological strangulation. Growing Sunday Schools must have classrooms if they continue to grow. But Christian educators differ in their conclusions as to how much room there must be for Sunday School growth. The traditional laws call for 10 square feet

CHART FOR GRADING SUNDAY SCHOOLS

CLOSELY GRADED PLAN

Find Your Present Enrollment And Grade To Grow	CRADLE ROLL (To 2 Years)	NURSERY (2-3 Years)	KINDER-GARTEN (4-5 Years)	PRIMARY (Ages 6-7-8)			JUNIOR (Ages 9-10-11)		
250 AND UP	Use Cradle Roll Kit	Use Nursery Lessons	Use Kinder-garten Lessons	Grade 1 Use First Grade Lessons	Grade 2 Use Second Grade Lessons	Grade 3 Use Third Grade Lessons	Grade 4 Use Fourth Grade Lessons	Grade 5 Use Fifth Grade Lessons	Grade 6 Use Sixth Grade Lessons
200 TO 250	Use Cradle Roll Kit	Use Nursery Lessons	Use Kinder-garten Lessons	Grade 1 Use First Grade Lessons	Grade 2 Use Second Grade Lessons	Grade 3 Use Third Grade Lessons	Grade 4 Use Fourth Grade Lessons	Grade 5 Use Fifth Grade Lessons	Grade 6 Use Sixth Grade Lessons
150 TO 200	Use Cradle Roll Kit	Use Nursery Lessons	Use Kinder-garten Lessons	Grade 1 Use First Grade Lessons	Grade 2 Use Second Grade Lessons	Grade 3 Use Third Grade Lessons	Grade 4 Use Fourth Grade Lessons	Grade 5 Use Fifth Grade Lessons	Grade 6 Use Sixth Grade Lessons

DEPARTMENTAL GRADED PLAN

	CRADLE ROLL (1 to 2 Years)	NURSERY (2-3 Years)	KINDER-GARTEN (4-5 Years)	PRIMARY (Ages 6-7-8)		JUNIOR (Ages 9-10-11)	
100 TO 150	Use Cradle Roll Kit	Use Nursery Lessons	Use Kinder-garten Lessons	Grade 1 Use First Grade Lessons	Grades 2, 3 Begin with Second Grade Lessons And Rotate Through Third Grade	Grade 4 Use Fourth Grade Lessons	Grades 5, 6 Begin With Fifth Grade Lessons And Rotate Through Sixth Grade
LESS THAN 100	Use Cradle Roll Kit	Preschool Use Kindergarten Lessons		Combine Primary Lessons These books have been especially designed for the smallest church where it is necesary to combine primary grades into one class.		Grades 4, 5, 6 Begin With Fourth Grade Lessons And Rotate Through Fifth & Sixth Grades	

JUNIOR HIGH (Ages 12-13-14)			HIGH SCHOOL (Ages 15-16-17)			YOUNG PEOPLE (Ages 18-24)	ADULTS (Ages 25 up)
Grade 7 Use Seventh Grade Lessons	Grade 8 Use Eighth Grade Lessons	Grade 9 Use Ninth Grade Lessons	Grade 10 Use Tenth Grade Lessons	Grade 11 Use Eleventh Grade Lessons	Grade 12 Use Twelfth Grade Lessons	College Young Single Young Married Use Adult Bible Series	Graded Adults Women Men Mixed Use Adult Bible Series
Grade 7 Use Seventh Grade Lessons	Grade 8 Use Eighth Grade Lessons	Grade 9 Use Ninth Grade Lessons	Grade 10 Use Tenth Grade Lessons	Grades 11 & 12 Begin with Eleventh Grade Lessons And Rotate Through Twelfth Grade		College Young Single Young Married Use Adult Bible Series	Graded Adults Women Men Mixed Use Adult Bible Series
Grade 7 Use Seventh Grade Lessons	Grades 8 & 9 Begin With Eighth Grade Lessons And Rotate Through Ninth Grade		Grade 10 Use Tenth Grade Lessons	Grades 11 & 12 Begin with Eleventh Grade Lessons And Rotate Through Twelfth Grade		College Young Single Young Married Use Adult Bible Series	Graded Adults Women Men Mixed Use Adult Bible Series

JUNIOR HIGH (Ages 12-13-14)		HIGH SCHOOL (Ages 15-16-17)	YOUNG PEOPLE (Ages 18-24)	ADULTS (Ages 25 & Older)
Grade 7 Use Seventh Grade Lessons	Grades 8, 9 Begin With Eighth Grade Lessons And Rotate Through Ninth Grade	Grades 10, 11, 12 Begin With Tenth Grade Lessons And Rotate Through Eleventh & Twelfth	Use Adult Bible Series	
	Grades 7, 8, 9 Begin With Seventh Grade Lessons And Rotate Through Eighth and Ninth Grades	Grades 10 11,12 Or Combine Tenth with J.H. and Eleventh & Twelfth with Young People's Class Begin Tenth Grade Lessons Rotate Thru Eleventh & Twelfth	Use Adult Bible Series	

per pupil. Those who conduct an activity-centered Sunday School, however, must have 25 square feet per pupil. Your space and building will to some degree dictate your approach to Sunday School teaching.

STEP 30   The Law of Organized Outreach

The Sunday School must be organized for growth. Since teaching is meeting needs, the Sunday School should be divided by ages to gather the common needs of the pupils into a unit for effective teaching. This is also referred to by Christian educators as grading the Sunday School. Grading recognizes certain natural sociological groups which will aid the teacher in teaching his class and become the basis for adding new classes. The chart on pages 44-45 is a typical organizational structure for the Sunday School. Depending on local conditions, the suggested age and/or grade groupings might be altered slightly.

6

RECOGNIZING THREE DANGER LEVELS OF GROWTH

How large is the typical American church? Statistically, the average American church has 87 people attending its Sunday morning worship service. A typical Sunday School runs 24 percent less than the morning service. This means the average Sunday School has about 66 in attendance on a typical Sunday. A study of Southern Baptist churches concluded the average attendance in their Sunday Schools was 64.7, almost 65 in attendance on a typical Sunday. (Most people think the Sunday School is larger but they forget the low attendance on holidays and summer pulls the average down.)

THE FIRST DANGER LEVEL— THE CLASS SUNDAY SCHOOL

STEP 31   Sunday Schools First Plateau at 100-150
The first danger level or plateau of Sunday School growth comes when attendance reaches beyond the average and stops growing at 100-150. This type of Sunday School is called the "one-room" Sunday School or the class Sunday School. That is because everything is organized around individual classes, or

47

they meet in the auditorium (one room) for opening exercises or opening worship. Just like a houseplant will outgrow the pot in which it was planted as it grows, so the number of pupils will outgrow the facilities and organizational structure as it grows. If the Sunday School is not reorganized to take care of more pupils, both the plant and Sunday School will become "root bound" and begin to die without growth. A root-bound plant chokes on its own roots

Why do Sunday Schools get "root bound" at the 100-150 plateau? There are three primary reasons. First, they simply run out of space or classrooms. New classes cannot be started for growth because there is no space. Remember the problem of sociological strangulation? A building is full when it is about 80 percent full. This means buildings which can seat 125-200 people comfortably will get root bound as they approach this first danger level.

The second reason for this natural plateau in growth is related to the basic management principle of span and direction. One manager should never have more than 7 people reporting to him. A superintendent cannot give effective direction, nor take

THE ONE-ROOM SUNDAY SCHOOL
Cradle roll (nursery)
Toddlers
Preschool
Primary (first grade)
Primary (second and third grade)
Junior Boys
Junior Girls
Young Teens (Junior High or Middle School)
High School
College and Career
Couples Class
Men's Class
Women's Class
Senior Saints (men)
Senior Saints (women)

responsibility for more than this amount of workers. By the time the class Sunday School has reached 100-150, the Sunday School superintendent is probably trying to manage 10 to 15 teachers and everyone begins to wonder why so many details are falling between the cracks.

A third reason for this danger level of 100 to 150 is that when the average Sunday School reaches this level, the leaders usually cannot think of other new classes to begin. The following 15 classes multiplied by 10 represents the upper danger level of Sunday School growth. (This division is not necessarily recommended but usually has evolved in the class or one-room Sunday School.)

This danger level is perhaps the most serious simply because it is the one which so many churches face in their present situation. There are steps that can be taken to break the "100" danger level. The Sunday School should probably consider changing its organizational structure to a departmentally organized Sunday School. Also, the church may need to find more room to grow. But the real key to breaking this danger level is to begin new classes.

HOW TO BREAK THE 100-150 BARRIER
1 Begin new classes.
2 Add additional administrators.
3 Find additional space for new classrooms (perhaps off campus).
4 Consider going to a split-level Sunday School.
5 Change large classes taught by one teacher into a team-teaching situation with several teachers.
6 Organize large classes or team-taught classes into a department.
7 Appoint one teacher as a departmental superintendent to supervise/coordinate the other teachers.

HOW TO BEGIN A NEW CLASS

STEP 32   Recruit a Teacher
The first step in beginning a new class is to find and recruit a teacher. Remember, you are looking for more than a person with teaching skills. You are looking for someone to lead the class. A spirit-filled Sunday School teacher can revitalize a class and ultimately a church. Whenever God did something significant in Scripture, He began first by calling out a person who would be the instrument by which He would accomplish His purpose. When He chose to create a race, He began with Adam. When He later had to destroy that race for its sin, He found Noah through whom He could preserve that which was worth saving. When He wanted a witness to the Gentile nations, there was an Abraham. When Israel was to be delivered from the land of Egypt, God found a Moses. As Israel prepared to enter the Promised Land, a general named Joshua was charged with the responsibility of conquest. Later there would be other judges, kings, and prophets whom God would raise up as He prepared to do new things in Israel.

In the New Testament, the pattern remained the same. There was a John "sent by God" to be the forerunner to the Messiah. Jesus chose to devote the majority of His ministry in investing His life into the lives of the Twelve who carried His message to the world. On the Day of Pentecost, there was a preacher named Peter. Before the Sanhedrin, there was Stephen. In Samaria, there was Philip. In other cities there would be Paul, Barnabas, Apollos, men of God sent by God to do the work of God.

In the history of the church since then, God has apparently not changed His strategy. In Germany, God's man was Luther. In France, it was Calvin. There was Zwingli in the Swiss Canton of Zurich, Knox in the Highlands of Scotland, Simons in the lowlands of Holland, and men with names like Hus, Wycliffe, Tyndale, and Wesley in the Isle of England. Their times and cultures, and to some extent even their theologies, were different, but each was God's man in God's place doing God's work at

God's time. There is no reason today to suspect God has changed this strategy which has worked so well for so long.

One of the most difficult tasks in leadership is recruiting teachers. First, don't try to talk people into teaching who don't have the spiritual gift of teaching. Begin by emphasizing that every person has a gift and should be using his gift for service. Second, give a spiritual gift inventory to help people discover their gift. Then recruit those with the spiritual gift of teaching for the task.

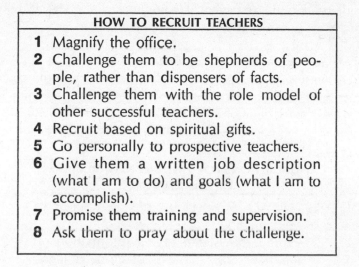

HOW TO RECRUIT TEACHERS
1 Magnify the office.
2 Challenge them to be shepherds of people, rather than dispensers of facts.
3 Challenge them with the role model of other successful teachers.
4 Recruit based on spiritual gifts.
5 Go personally to prospective teachers.
6 Give them a written job description (what I am to do) and goals (what I am to accomplish).
7 Promise them training and supervision.
8 Ask them to pray about the challenge.

STEP 33   Get Seed Members

The second step in beginning a new class is to get some seed members to help the new teacher get the class started. Sometimes seed members come from dividing a class. Do not divide a class too often because this tends to discourage members who rebuild their class only to be divided again. It is difficult to begin a new class with just a teacher. When the teacher goes into an empty room, he can become discouraged and quit. However, if he has a core of people to help him build the class, he is less likely to get discouraged.

STEP 34 Find a Room

The biggest problem for some churches in beginning a new class is finding a room for the class. This problem is not insurmountable, even if you are already using the pastor's study and several halls and Sunday School buses in the parking lot. More and more Sunday School classes are meeting off campus than ever before. Classes are meeting in homes, schools, restaurants, and many other nontraditional settings. Don Crane, pastor of Faith Baptist Church, Richmond, Virginia, began meeting with 2 single adults in a booth in a restaurant for Sunday morning breakfast and Bible study. They grew into 35 single adults meeting in a side room of the restaurant. Finding room for a new class does not always mean a new building program.

STEP 35 Expand the Organization

To begin new classes, leaders need to get others in the church to accept their existence. Expansion begins by accepting the goal and contribution of new classes and supporting them. If the new class is an open class, then other teachers may view it as a

---

SUGGESTIONS FOR FINDING NEW MEMBERS FOR THE NEW CLASS

1 Gather a prospect list of F.R.A.N.s from seed members.

2 Write a newsletter giving information on the new class (goals, location, officers, first lesson series, names of seed members).

3 Appoint an outreach leader to be responsible for leading the class to contact prospects.

4 Announcements in the church should feature the outreach potential of the class, not just its teaching potential. As a result, members may have prospects for the new class, or they may want to join the class.

threat either to take away members or be in competition to recruit potential members.

Next, expand by appointing class officers for the new class to help in reaching others with the Gospel. Finally, the ushers, secretaries, and other administrators in the Sunday School will need to know of the existence of the new class and how it fits into the scheme of things.

STEP 36   Go After People

Ultimately, beginning a new class will involve going out after new people. As noted earlier, there is only one way to build a church. That way is through reaching new members. Within that one way, there are many strategies and steps.

THE SECOND DANGER LEVEL— THE DEPARTMENTAL SUNDAY SCHOOL

STEP 37   Sunday School's Second Plateau: 250-350

The second danger level or natural plateau in Sunday School growth occurs as attendance averages 250-350. This is the upper limit of the departmental Sunday School. In this Sunday School, everything is organized around the departmental structure. Because the average department has 40 pupils, eight full departments have 320 pupils. Sunday Schools which have broken through the 100-150 barrier have usually switched from classes to a graded Sunday School organized around departments (see charts on pages 54-55).

THE THIRD DANGER LEVEL— THE AGE-GRADED SUNDAY SCHOOL

STEP 38   Sunday School's Third Plateau: 750-1,000

The third danger level plateau of Sunday School growth occurs as Sunday Schools average 750-1,000. This is the upper limit of growth in the closely graded Sunday School. A closely graded Sunday School adds a department (40 average) for each age in the school grades and a department of adults (each class division

SUNDAY SCHOOL ORGANIZATION CHART

AGE	0-1	2-3	4-5	6-7-8	9-10-11
GRADE				1 2 3	4 5 6
CLASS-GRADED Sunday School Attendance: 100	(Nursery Care 0-1)	Preschool Class	Kindergarten Class	Primary Class	Junior Class (Boys and Girls together)
Percent of Attendance	7%		8%	15%	18%
DEPARTMENTALLY GRADED Sunday School Attendance: 250-350	Cribs & Toddlers	2 Preschool Classes	Open Session One Room 4 tables — — — — — Traditional 1 Dept. 4 classes	Open Session One Room 6 tables — — — — — Traditional 1 Dept. 6 classes	Open Session One Room 6 tables — — — — — Traditional 1 Dept. 6 classes
AGE-GRADED Sunday School Attendance: 400-1,000	4 Nurseries	4 Preschool Classes	Open Session Rooms Open Class for each Age Level 6 tables per classroom	Open Session Rooms One Class for each Age Level 8-9 tables per classroom	

12-13-14	15-16-17	18-24	25-60	Senior Citizen	
7 8 9	10 11 12	College			
Junior High Class	High School Class	Young Adults	Adult Class	Women's Class	Men's Class
12%		40%			
Junior High Dept. 7th Grade Class 8th Grade Class 9th Grade Class	High School Dept. 10th Grade Class 11th Grade Class 12th Grade Class	College-Career Young Married Special Classes	Adult Dept. Organized Electives Age-Graded	Women's Classes	Men's Classes
One Class per Age Level 5-7 workers for each class		Classes organized for each Age Level of adults			

of five years, as an illustration, a men's class age 30 to 34).

I first listed the 100 largest Sunday Schools in America in 1967 in the annual *Christian Life* magazine listing. There were only 97 Sunday Schools in America that averaged more than 1,000 at that time. But I felt there were going to be a great number of them so I predicted that the decade of the '70s would be the decade of the super church or the mega church. Time has seen it come about. Twenty years later, Dr. John Vaughan, Professor of Church Growth at Southwest Baptist University, Boliver, Missouri, has listed 8,160 churches averaging over 1,000. In 20 years the number grew from 97 to 8,160.

STEP 39 New Classes Cause Growth

Sunday Schools grow through the adding of new classes, departments, or new areas of outreach. First, classes must be organized for outreach. Then when visitors come to the Sunday School, there is structure to help keep them. A Sunday School cannot sustain growth without new classes. To grow by 100, a total of 10 new classes must be added to the Sunday School.

STEP 40 Add or Divide Classes

The traditional approach, to divide classes in order to grow, is not the only foundation for expansion. New classes can be added without cutting into existing classes (see steps 32-36). The division of classes and creation of new classes in and by itself does not provide motivation to grow. Growth comes from an evangelistic spirit and a desire to reach people for Christ. Growth comes from a dynamic spirit that grows out of a "people-oriented" Sunday School.

The traditional phrase was "divide and multiply." New classes can be added without the disadvantages associated with breaking up a good and growing class. Or, when lethargy sets in, dividing a class becomes a step to growth.

STEP 41 The Church Body Grows Like the Physical Body

The first time I visited Dr. Paul Youngi Cho, pastor of the largest church in the world, the Full-Gospel Church of Seoul,

Korea, was in 1978. We discussed the laws of Sunday School growth. He told me he had read about the laws in my books but claimed, "If I followed the laws I could not have grown and if I followed them now, I would quit growing."

Dr. Cho explained that (in 1978) he had 160,000 in his church and that he would have had to build a Sunday School building four times the size of U.C.L.A. (University of California, Los Angeles) to house them all. U.C.L.A. had 40,000 students, one fourth of the 160,000 people in his church. Cho went on to explain that if he did build that large in the past, then he could not afford to build in the future and would stop growing.

Dr. Cho explained that he grew his church by cell groups meeting in homes during the week.

Dr. Cho used the illustration of the physical body as an analogy for the church body. He said Koreans understood this analogy better than Westerners, "A body is formed when the life of the man in his seed joins to the life of the woman in her egg and produces a cell."

Cho held his fingers so they almost touched and said, "The cell is so small you cannot see it with the natural eye. But all the characteristics of the new baby are in this cell, whether blond hair, black hair, or," looking at me he added, "bald.

"If the cell grows it is diseased and is discharged," he explained. "The fertilization process must start again.

"A cell does not grow. Growth comes from the cell dividing. Then both cells are identical. You cannot tell which cell began first. Each cell divides making two cells, then four cells. Then they divide into eight cells; the process is unending. When cells stop dividing, death takes place."

I received insight into church growth when Cho then said, "The body grows by the division of cells."

I then realized the church—the local body of Christ—grew by the division of cells or classes and departments. Cho was right about Korean church growth; it came as he divided his home Bible study cells for growth. But Cho was also wrong. American Sunday School classes had never grown because of classrooms. American Sunday Schools followed the same principles; they grew by the division of classes.

The secret of Sunday School growth is adding ministries, adding ministers, and adding places of ministry. We must add classes, add teachers, and expand our base for growth.

SECRET OF GROWTH
Add Ministries
Add Ministers
Add Places of Ministry

If a physical cell grows without division in the physical body, it becomes cancer. By the same principle, cancer happens in the body of Christ. When cells do not divide, and new ministries are not added, spiritual cancer sets in the local church.

7

RECOGNIZING THE DIFFERENCES IN EVANGELISM

STEP 42   Use Front Door Evangelism
Evangelism is communicating the Gospel to people in an understandable way and motivating people to respond to Christ and become a member of His church. There are several ways in which churches have expressed evangelism in recent years. Perhaps the most common of these is "Front Door Evangelism," also called "Inviting Evangelism" because it centers around inviting people to enter through the front door of the church where they can hear the Gospel in an event and be saved. This is also called "Event Evangelism." The event can be a Sunday morning preaching service or an evangelistic service where evangelism happens. One problem with event evangelism is that the stained-glass barrier will keep many from entering the building so they can be evangelized. In spite of its limitations, Front Door Evangelism is where most evangelism happens.

STEP 43 Use Saturation Evangelism
A second type of evangelism is "Saturation Evangelism" or "Media Evangelism." This kind of evangelism has been defined as, "using every available means to reach every available person at every available time." The biblical basis of saturation evangelism

is described where the early church had saturated Jerusalem with the Gospel as a lawn is saturated with water. They had gone house to house and preached publicly in the temple (Acts 5:42). As a result the opposition said, "Look, you have filled Jerusalem with your doctrine, and intend to bring this Man's blood on us!" (Acts 5:28)

SIDE DOOR EVANGELISM

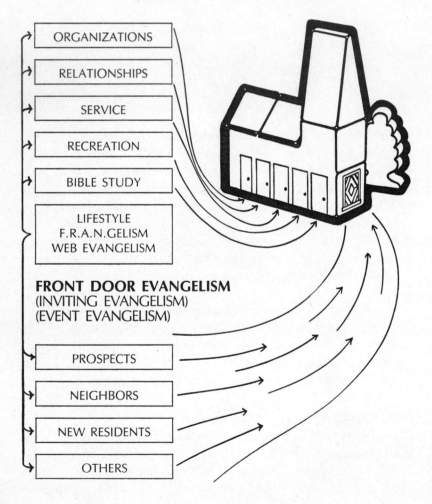

ORGANIZATIONS

RELATIONSHIPS

SERVICE

RECREATION

BIBLE STUDY

LIFESTYLE
F.R.A.N.GELISM
WEB EVANGELISM

FRONT DOOR EVANGELISM
(INVITING EVANGELISM)
(EVENT EVANGELISM)

PROSPECTS

NEIGHBORS

NEW RESIDENTS

OTHERS

STEP 44 Use Media for Evangelism

While many will do evangelism only as described in the Bible, one pastor said he would go a step farther and use any evangelistic method not expressly forbidden in Scripture so he could reach people with the Gospel. This includes (a) busing, (b) campaigns, (c) advertising, (d) cassettes, (e) newspapers, (f) newsletters, (g) radio announcements, (h) television, (i) flyers, and (j) billboards.

In 1971, I was Sunday School Superintendent at Thomas Road Baptist Church, Lynchburg, Virginia when Sunday School attendance averaged approximately 4,000 a week. Pastor Jerry Falwell set an attendance goal of 10,000, an unheard of record attendance. The goal was to saturate the city and surrounding counties. First, all 103 pages of the telephone book were distributed to 103 volunteers with the instruction to phone everyone and invite them to Sunday School. Twelve billboards surrounding the city invited visitors to the service. Sixty radio announcements were played on every station and 10 announcements on the 1 television station invited people to Sunday School. A flyer was placed under the windshield wiper of every automobile in town and 5,000 posters were tacked on trees, light poles, etc. Three mailings (a letter, flyer, and post card) were sent to every home in a 5 county area. Finally, 200 workers went door to door on the Saturday before the big day to invite visitors to Sunday School. As a result of saturating our "Jerusalem," 10,154 attended Harvest Day, 1972.

But by 1987, Dr. Falwell was qualifying his opinion on every phase of Saturation Evangelism. He said it didn't work as it used to work because of the high price of media. Falwell was exhorting "Back to Basics," which included visiting, contacting friends, working through Sunday School teachers, etc.

STEP 45 Be Superaggressive in Outreach

"Superaggressive Evangelism" is not a method, it is an attitude that the Christian should have in being energetic and innovative in giving the Gospel to every person. Often the terms "superaggressive evangelism" and "saturation evangelism" are used interchangeably. However, they do have different emphases. When speaking of saturation evangelism, we are emphasizing the means by which the Great Commission is accomplished. Superaggressive refers more to the attitude of faith and obedience with which the task is done.

If everyone is lost and needs Christ as Saviour, and if the Great Commission demands that the Gospel be given to everyone, then the church should be aggressive in obedience, aggressive in faith, and superaggressive in method. The key to understanding superaggressive evangelism is to possess, or rather be possessed by a vision of what God can do.

WHY PEOPLE CHOOSE A SUNDAY SCHOOL CLASS

In order to attempt to get pupils into your Sunday School class, you should examine the reasons why people have joined the class in the past. The past motivations that attracted visitors to the class is an excellent door through which you should attempt to attract future visitors to your class.

My students at Liberty University have done a number of local church surveys in which they question new members of a Sunday School class asking why they chose that particular class. Leaders of growing Sunday Schools need to know how the unchurched "think" about coming to Bible study so they can use the same appeal in successfully inviting other unchurched people to Sunday School. Too many leaders base their outreach to the unchurched on what "they" desire, rather than on the needs of the unchurched.

BUILDING YOUR CLASS OF FRIENDSHIPS
1 Provide coffee time for fellowship.
2 A host/hostess to greet everyone.
3 Name tags.
4 Use the principles of Friend Day.
5 Allow time for testimonies/sharing.

STEP 46   The Unchurched Are Looking for Fellowship

The primary reason unchurched people gave for attending a Sunday School was they were looking for fellowship or they attended with a friend. It was a desire for an existing relationship which motivated them to choose a Sunday School class.

STEP 47   The Unchurched Are Looking for Help

A second reason why people say they attend a class is because they are looking for help. The lesson should meet a real or felt need in their lives. Some may want help with a habit or job problem. In one church, a significant number of students chose to attend a class that dealt almost exclusively with resolving marriage and family life related problems. In my class I used the following lessons in April-May 1987 to attract people to my adult Bible class.

LESSONS TO HELP PEOPLE
How to make decisions.
How not to make wrong decisions.
Lesser-known gifts and applying them to your life.
How to celebrate your birthday.
How to get a raise.
How to get the most out of your vacation.

STEP 48   People Choose Topic, Teacher, and Method

The third reason people choose a particular Sunday School class relates to their interest in (1) the topic, (2) the personality of the teacher, or (3) the predominant teaching method used in the class (discussion, films, question and answer). As an illustration, a person attends a class on prophecy because he may be interested in learning the identity of the Antichrist. Others might attend a class because they enjoy the teacher's humor or enjoy the way he stimulates discussions. Another person may attend a class because he likes the method, which means he can be involved in the weekly discussion, or he enjoys the question and answer approach to teaching.

STEP 49   Use Side Door Evangelism

In contrast to "Front Door" approaches to evangelism, "Side Door Evangelism" is first networking people with church members, second, networking them into the activities of the church, and third, through these relationships, networking a person to Jesus Christ. More people come into the church through contacts with members of the church than they do through an advertising campaign that attracts them through the front door of the church. Statistically, far more people attend a church as the result of an invitation of a friend or relative than any other means by which people are attracted to the church. In hundreds of opinion polls I have conducted in churches and seminars across the country, I have found about 2 percent of those surveyed are drawn to the church through some form of church advertising. This is media evangelism which has an impersonal outreach. About 6 percent tend to credit the influence of the pastor in making their decision for Christ or joining a particular church. Another 6 percent credit the efforts of an organized church outreach team in bringing them to Christ or attracting them to the church. This could be described as soul-winning visitation, bus visitation, or an evangelistic team. The remaining 86 percent of those surveyed claim they were primarily influenced in their decision for Christ or choosing a church by the influence of a friend or relative.

This is one of the reasons why the "Friend Day Campaign" has been so successful for the more than 15,000 churches which have purchased the campaign from Church Growth Institute (by 1987). Untold numbers of churches have conducted a "Friend Day" without purchasing the campaign materials. One of the greatest potentials for outreach of a Sunday School is by reaching the friends of pupils who already come. Because these friends know and trust those who already come to Sunday School, there is a better possibility that they may attend and respond to the Word of God. As a matter of fact, if everyone

WHY FRIEND DAY IS SUCCESSFUL
1 An Enrolling Campaign—F.R.A.N.s commit themselves on paper to attend.
2 A Credible Campaign—the leaders (pastor, board, teachers) become examples to the members.
3 A Networking Campaign—visitors attend the service because of their relationship to a member.
4 A Stair-Stepping Campaign—members do not attempt to get decisions for Christ up front, but influence their F.R.A.N.s one step at a time.
5 A First-Step Campaign—those who make a first-step commitment to attend will have an easier time making a final-step commitment to Christ.
6 A Quality Prospect Campaign—F.R.A.N.s of members will be most responsive to your church and most receptive to the Gospel.
7 A Low Budget Campaign—no cost for evangelist, motel, meals, and low cost for advertisement.

brought only one friend, a Sunday School could double its outreach.

Of course, there is a right way and a wrong way to get your pupils to reach their friends for Christ. Many have tried the quick announcement heard at the end of the lesson, "Everyone invite a friend for next week." If everyone followed the advice, Sunday School attendance would double the following week. The idea is good, but that approach just doesn't work because the suggestion lacks "believability." However, a planned "Friend Day" will work because it builds credibility into the Sunday

School pupils. The leader demonstrates credibility in the program by showing to the church a letter from someone who will be his friend and will attend with him on Friend Day.

The "Friend Day Campaign" takes a full month to build credibility so that every member will bring a friend to church. During the course of the campaign, specially prepared lessons teach the value of friends and friendship. The first week of the campaign, the pastor announces his friend to the congregation and reads a letter from his friend promising to attend on "Friend Day." The next week, members of the official church board read letters from their friends. On the third Sunday of the campaign, every teacher has a "Friendly Contract" completed by his friend who promises to come on "Friend Day." The next week, every member is asked to turn in their "Friendly Contracts" in preparation for "Friend Day" the following Sunday.

STEP 50   Use Lifestyle Evangelism
In contrast to the above mentioned "Front Door" and "Side Door" approach to evangelism, many Christians and churches are engaged in one or more approaches to evangelism that are not generally related to the church. One of these strategies is called "Lifestyle Evangelism," which is a reaction to what has been called "Personal Evangelism." This is the style of evangelism that is usually taught in courses on soul-winning. Personal evangelism is usually (1) confrontational, (2) verbal, giving the plan of salvation, (3) nonchurch related, and (4) stranger-oriented. Lifestyle Evangelism swings to the other side emphasizing (1) nonconfrontational sharing, (2) nonverbal, (3) friendship-oriented, but it is (4) nonchurch related.

The basic premise of Lifestyle Evangelism is that the unsaved must know more than the words of the Gospel, because Gospel orthodoxy never saved anyone. Your style of life will win them to Christ. First, they must see its message in you. Second, because of your role-model they will desire to have the same kind of life. But in the third place, they will see Christ in you, then identify with Him and accept Him into their lives. It is built on a valid premise that the lifestyle of every Christian should be a witness for Jesus Christ (Acts 1:8).

Most books on personal evangelism are confrontational in nature, designed to help Christians lead others to a decision to accept Jesus Christ. This approach to evangelism scares some Christians from evangelism because they are not confrontational in their lifestyles. Lifestyle evangelism allows them to use their nonverbal testimony to influence others for Christ. Some have attacked lifestyle evangelism because they feel it is too passive for their approach to evangelism. However, do not place a qualitative (right or wrong) judgment on lifestyle evangelism, look at it quantitatively. It is not the most effective approach to evangelism, but it has a place and has some influence.

STEP 51 Share Your Testimony

"Testimony Evangelism" can be used in a "side door" approach to evangelism. This is verbal evangelism where the believer shares his experience. Some Christians cannot give the plan of salvation to a lost person. They think that is preaching or they think that is salesmanship. But everyone can tell what has happened to them. Testimony evangelism is sharing our experience in Jesus Christ with other people so that they too will want to experience what we have in Christ.

STEP 52 Share What You Have Seen

First, a witness should share what he has seen about Jesus Christ, "That which was from the beginning . . . which we have seen with our eyes, which we have looked upon" (1 John 1:1).

There are two areas that we want to share as a result of our looking. First, what we have seen in Jesus Christ. The two disciples on the Road to Emmaus were first blinded to Christ, but He gave them spiritual sight. The Bible says "their eyes were opened" (Luke 24:31) and they knew Him. When we know Christ, we want to share Him with our friends.

In the second place we see a difference in our lives. We see how our desires have changed and our lives are different. Then we want to share with our friends what Christ has done for us.

STEP 53 Share What You Have Heard

A witness should share what he has heard about Jesus Christ. When Peter and John were called before the Sanhedrin for their preaching, they confessed, "For we cannot but speak the things which we have seen and heard" (Acts 4:20).

STEP 54 Share What You Have Experienced

When a person is called as a witness in a legal trial, the judge will not permit his opinion, only what he has seen, heard, or experienced. A witness should share what he has experienced in his relationship with Jesus Christ. In Acts 4:1-20, a healed man who had been lame from birth stood with Peter and John. He gave his testimony as to what had happened to him, "And seeing the man who had been healed standing with them, they could say nothing against it" (v. 14). Testimony evangelism is an effective evangelistic strategy because it gives credibility to the message.

STEP 55 Network the Unchurched through Relationships

F.R.A.N.gelism or "Friendship Evangelism" is a "side door" evangelistic strategy that networks people to Christ and His church through relationships. The foundation of modern Sunday School growth is through relationship evangelism, people bringing their F.R.A.N.s to church. (The acronym F.R.A.N. is also applied to a campaign similar to Friend Day called F.R.A.N.tastic Days.) This approach is also called Web Evangelism because we can evangelize through web relationships. Those reached through web relationships tend to be easier to bond to the church. This enables the church not only to reach the lost but also experience numerical growth because their converts stick.

STEP 56 Don't Give up on Sunday School Busing

"Bus Evangelism" is a method of establishing a bus route and visiting people along that route to invite them to attend the Sunday School with a view of reaching them for Christ. It is more than convenience busing, it is intentional evangelism, using a bus as a tool to reach people. Bus Evangelism has been declining in recent years but is now stabilized. The reason Sunday School busing has declined is because of increased cost of gasoline, insurance, and maintenance on the vehicles. Some churches got into the bus ministry for the wrong reasons (just for numbers, or to keep their children from going to other churches). The high cost of running buses has been enough to force these churches out of the bus ministry. Also, the nurturing aim of some Sunday Schools was at cross points with the implied evangelistic nature of bus ministry.

STEP 57   Busing Will Revitalize a Dead Sunday School
Every church should consider running at least one Sunday School bus as part of its total evangelistic strategy. A bus ministry will bring outreach, soul-winning, and excitement into the church. If the bus workers reach out in faith, it could bring revival to the church.

STEP 58   Busing Leads to Soul-Winning
Those opposed to busing will question if the church really wants all the excitement associated with Sunday School busing when "bus kids" damage the church property and facilities, get into fights with the church leaders' kids, and stuff rolls of toilet paper down the commode Sunday morning. Look beyond the problems. The real excitement of bus ministry is when children are actually won to Jesus Christ. When that happens, there is not only rejoicing in heaven, but also among the bus and Sunday School workers who are involved in bringing boys and girls to a saving knowledge of Christ through this ministry.

STEP 59   Busing Reaches Parents Through Side Door Evangelism
Busing is an excellent tool for reaching families for Christ. After the child who rides the bus is won to Christ, the workers can use that leverage to reach his parents. Through side door evangelism families are brought into the church.

8

F.R.A.N.GELISM

STEP 60   Reach Friends

One of the most exciting trends in evangelistic outreach today is an outreach program called "F.R.A.N.GELISM."¹ Nothing like the exciting outreach of Friendship Evangelism has stirred churches to outreach since the busing explosion of the early '70s. It's new, it's exciting, and it is getting results. It's new in the sense that Friendship Evangelism has not been organized and emphasized, though it has been used. But now a sleeping giant is stirring. A strategy of evangelism as old as Andrew bringing his brother Peter to Christ is now being rediscovered and applied by an army of lay evangelists across the land. This program is a tool by which church members reach the unchurched by reaching those in their circles of concern or spheres of influence.

The word "F.R.A.N.GELISM" is in part an acrostic. The "F" in F.R.A.N.GELISM represents "friends."

STEP 61   Reach Relatives

The "R" in F.R.A.N.GELISM represents another sphere of influence, "relatives." Sometimes F.R.A.N.gelism or Web Evangelism has been described as "Oikos Evangelism." The Greek term *oikos* is translated family, household, or others. Technically, *oikos* included (1) the close blood family, (2) the extended blood family (those related but not necessarily living under the same roof), and (3) those who are part of the family and participate in the family but not related (in the New Testament this included slaves and/or neighbors). Salvation was offered to the household (*oikos*) of the Philippian jailer (Acts 16:31) plus the *oikos* of Zaccheus, the demoniac of the Gadarenes, and Cornelius. The Bible emphasizes the family/relatives as a major target area of salvation.

STEP 62   Reach Associates

The "A" in F. R. A. N. GELISM represents another group of people in our circles of concern, "associates." These are business associates, plus those on bowling teams, volunteer fire squads, community service groups, and any other relationship that puts us in contact with the unchurched. The believer should have a witness (Lifestyle Evangelism) and give his testimony to his associates, forming a basis for reaching them for Christ.

STEP 63   Reach Neighbors

The "N" in F. R. A. N. GELISM represents our "neighbors." These neighbors may represent relatives, friends, or associates, but they are targeted because they live near a believer or near the church. They are more than a prospect (an unchurched person), because they are a neighbor with a relation to you, they are a receptive-responsive person to the Gospel.

STEP 64   Use Your Spiritual Gifts Properly for Outreach[2]

F. R. A. N. GELISM is a program designed to involve all people and all spiritual gifts in the evangelistic outreach of the local church. The key to the success of this program is found in using people where they are usable.

Using people where they are usable is another way of saying, "Get every church member involved in ministry according to his spiritual gift."

Three basic facts about spiritual gifts immediately affect all

Christians in your church. First, every Christian has at least one spiritual gift (1 Cor. 7:7). Second, every Christian ought to know his spiritual gift (12:1). Third, every Christian ought to be serving Christ with his spiritual gift (Rom. 12:6-8).

Not everyone has the gift of evangelism. Paul indicates only some have the gift, "some evangelists" (Eph. 4:11). This does not mean others are excluded from soul-winning, nor does it mean they can't be used in reaching the lost. All are commanded to be witnesses (Acts 1:8), and to all has been committed the word of reconciliation (2 Cor. 5:19-20), so that all are ambassadors for Christ.

Rather than try to make all Christians function as though they had the gift of evangelism, Friendship Evangelism is designed to help each believer discover and develop his/her individual spiritual gifts and apply them in doing the work of evangelism. Christians should serve in those capacities for which God has specifically and uniquely gifted them. In Proverbs 18:16, Solomon wrote, "A man's gift makes room for him, and brings him before great men."

Any adequate definition of spiritual gifts must address at least three vital areas: the source of spiritual gifts, the nature of spiritual gifts, and the purpose of spiritual gifts. Therefore, *a spiritual gift is a special ability given by the Holy Spirit to enable Christians to do productive service in the body of Christ.* This brief definition addresses three key issues. (1) The Holy Spirit is the source of the spiritual gifts, (2) "special ability" speaks of their nature, and (3) "service" speaks of the purpose of the gifts.

Scripture addresses those same three key issues. Paul spoke of gifts as being "the manifestation of the Spirit" (1 Cor. 12:7, which tells the source). Peter made clear the nature of spiritual gifts, when he wrote, "If anyone ministers, let him do it as with the ability which God supplies" (1 Peter 4:11). Again in the first Corinthian letter, Paul indicated that the purpose of gifts is Christian service (1 Cor. 12:7, 25).

A program of F.R.A.N.GELISM divides workers into four general tasks, representing four areas of spiritual gifts: (1) evangelists, (2) equippers, (3) encouragers, (4) helpers.

Evangelists present the Gospel to unsaved in their homes. Others are employed as equippers or educators who disciple the new converts into the church. Then there are the encouragers with the gift of showing mercy. These people visit the shut-in, absentee, sick, and those with a spiritual problem to encourage them to be faithful. Encouragers are ready to help them resolve their problems. A fourth group involved with F. R. A. N. GELISM are the helpers and intercessors who support the outreach program in prayer and by caring for details behind the scenes. These people run the program of F. R. A. N. GELISM and insure its success.

Skyline Wesleyan Church, Lemon Grove, California is Friendship Evangelism in action. Attendance more than doubled in five years (1973-78), growing from 1,000 to over 2,800. In spite of having an auditorium that seats only 900, they have continued to evangelize.

Wednesday night is outreach night. Approximately 250 gather for a fellowship meal; then, around the dinner table, Pastor Maxwell challenges them for the ministry of the evening. He trains them so they can disciple others.

The 250 people represent several groups. First a group of ladies prepares the meal. This is their way of being included in the outreach program. A lady who had cooked for the church all her life told Pastor Maxwell, "I want to thank you for letting me be a part of reaching people for Christ." She had used her cooking talents in the past, but now she felt that service was part of a greater task—outreach.

There is a group of helpers. They keep the records (basic data on prospects, sick calls, new converts to follow-up, absentees, those with special problems, etc.). These helpers look after the records, getting the right person to do the right thing at the right time.

A second group (we call them evangelists) are given the names of prospects to visit that evening. Because they have the gift of evangelism they want to meet strangers and present the Gospel to them. They are usually good at it because it is their spiritual gift. They probably have more success than those who go visiting from other churches, because they are going to see prospects who have visited the church. The prospects (receptive-responsive people) they go to see usually have a relationship with someone in the church. Hence, because they present the Gospel to prospects with greater interest, they have a higher number of decisions for Christ.

A third group (we call them equippers) will be given the names of those who have joined the church or have made a recent public profession of salvation. The equippers meet with a new convert to disciple him in the faith. Equippers are not soulwinners, though they may have some success in that area. They are gifted to teach or shepherd people. They teach one-on-one, or two equippers meet with a couple. This discipling relationship exists for eight weeks, making sure the new convert is grounded in the faith and "bonded" to the church. After an equipper has finished the eight-week lesson, he is given another new convert to teach.

The fourth group (encouragers) are those with the spiritual gift of showing mercy (Rom. 12:8). They use their spiritual gift to encourage people. They are given a list of absentees who may need encouragement. Also, they are given the names of those who are sick, shut-in, or who have a special need. The encouragers are not expected to make soul-winning calls, though at times they may be directly responsible for leading people to Christ. As they encourage some and help others, they build the body. They allow the evangelist to give priority time to prospects. This allows both to be successful.

The last group (intercessors) pray support for the outreach ministry. When the evangelists, equippers, and encouragers leave at approximately 7 P.M., the intercessors go to prayer. The helpers give the intercessors the names of those who are prospects, new converts, and those who have special needs. The intercessors divide into smaller groups. Then, on their knees, they pray for specific people and for specific needs.

Through the drawing process, the prospect is brought into personal contact (networking) with several Christians. When the unsaved prospect comes to one of those difficult places where he is unable to make the next step toward the Lord, and a soul-winner can't seem to provide the needed answer, a word from another Christian may be just what is needed. The drawing process enables Christians to become laborers together with one another, as well as with God. The strengths of one believer can offset the weakness of others, and this is exactly as it should be (1 Cor. 3:6-8).

STEP 65   The Law of Three Hearings and Seven Touches
Two of the foundational principles that make F. R. A. N. GELISM work are expressed in the law of three hearings and the law of the seven touches. These two principles refer to the results of research into the successful evangelistic strategy of growing churches.

The Law of Three Hearings. Research shows that the average visitor to the church does not decide to accept Christ or join the church the first time he visits a church. A person will usually attend a church 3.4 times before making a meaningful decision to become a Christian or unite with the church. It is similar to a person purchasing a new suit or a new car; the more significant the purchase, the longer it takes some people to make up their mind. This does not mean that some are not saved the first time they visit a Gospel-preaching church. The time it takes to get someone saved depends on their receptivity to the Gospel and responsiveness to the church. The figure 3.4 is a statistical average and implies those who make a permanent decision for Christ usually attend church about three times before they decide to be saved.

The Law of Seven Touches. But it takes more than three hearings to get a permanent response to the Gospel. The unsaved must be networked into the church if he will remain true to the decision he makes for Christ. This means there must also be the law of the seven touches. Research shows that a person is more likely to return for the second and third visit if they are contacted seven times after their first visit. These contacts, or touches, can be initiated by the church through letters, phone calls, visits, or other personal contacts. These seven touches also include times the prospect sees the church message in the Yellow Pages, billboards, advertisements, flyers, or church newsletter. The obvious conclusion is that the church that contacts the most people the most times will probably have the greatest results. However, evangelistic results never depend on only one aspect, such as the number of contacts a church makes with a prospect or the number of hearings given to the Gospel. But when all aspects of evangelism are followed—including the laws of the three hearings and the seven touches—the more likely a person will respond to the Gospel.

A recent survey by the United Methodist Church indicates that if a layman (people perceive the pastor is paid to make the visit) will visit in the home of a first-time attender to a church within 36 hours (before Monday evening), there is an 80 percent likelihood the prospect will return the next Sunday. Also, the prospect will get a perspective of the church from a lay visit that he doesn't get from the pastor.

STEP 66   Target Receptive-Responsive People

Another reason for the success of F. R. A. N. GELISM is found in the effort to target receptive-responsive people. The old term was prospects, but the new term is receptive-responsive person. A prospect was usually identified as an unchurched family. But just because they are not identified with a church does not mean they are receptive to or can be reached with the Gospel. An evangelist should invest his time trying to evangelize those who are receptive-responsive people. When an evangelist goes from house to house, witnessing for Jesus Christ, he cannot get into most homes. Some people are nice to him, but usually they do not invite him into the home. Some are hostile to him because of his church or some other reason, while a few may be hostile to the Gospel. Hence, he has spent his energy with little results. House-to-house visitation should be restricted to canvass work that is designed to (1) make friends, (2) invite people to church, and (3) locate receptive-responsive people.

The ideal candidate for salvation is "receptive" to the soul-winner and "responsive" to the Gospel. While knocking on doors, every once in a while the soul-winner finds someone who is receptive to him. The soul-winner is invited into the home. When the Gospel is presented, the prospect receives Christ as Saviour, attends the church, is baptized, and goes on to serve Christ. But most door-to-door evangelism is nonproductive. When the evangelist makes most of his calls to receptive-responsive people, his harvest would be greater and more people would be won to Christ.

Through F. R. A. N. GELISM follow-up, the soul-winner knows those who are receptive to him and responsive to the Gospel. He can give priority time to those who are hungry for the Gospel.

Some people become receptive to both the messenger and the message. Naaman is the perfect example of receptivity (2 Kings 5:1, 9-14). He was a highly respected man of position, but he was a leper. Naaman went to Elisha, the prophet of God, in search of cleansing. Elisha sent a messenger to tell Naaman to go and wash in the Jordan River. Naaman was offended: first by the fact that Elisha sent a servant instead of coming himself, and second by the content of the message. In short, Naaman rejected both the messenger and the message.

When someone pointed out to Naaman that pride was standing in the way of his cleansing, he repented. He responded to the message and was cleansed. But Naaman was not responsive to the message until first he was receptive to the messenger. Receptivity is usually tied to responsiveness.

The degree of receptivity varies from one person to another. The most receptive people are usually those to whom a believer is closest. These are his friends, relatives, associates, and neighbors (F. R. A. N. s).

Jesus likened evangelism to sowing the seed of the Gospel in four different types of soil, representing four different types of people. He referred to the varying receptivity of the people in terms of four kinds of soil (Matt. 13:3-23).

First, the soil by the wayside represents those who were unreceptive. They hear the message and might be people who are receptive to the messenger but reject the message. Second, the seed in the stony soil without depth springs up immediately but dies because it lacks a root system. They represent people who superficially receive the message, but when tribulation or persecution arise because of the Word, they are offended and fall away. Third, the thorny soil illustrates those who are temporarily receptive, but they are unwilling to make the changes required of them. Fourth, the truly receptive are represented by the good ground. They respond and become fruitful.

The good soil brought forth fruit, thirtyfold, sixtyfold, and a hundredfold. The different amounts of fruitfulness indicate that people respond differently to the message of God.

The degree of receptivity will vary from one person to another. Among one's closest friends there are likely to be some who are indifferent, some who are receptive, and some who are totally unreceptive.

SCALE OF RECEPTIVITY		
Unreceptive	Indifferent	Receptive
-10 -8 -6 -4	-2 0 +2	+4 +6 +8 +10

Receptivity not only varies from person to person, but also from time to time. People change with the passage of time and the change of events. One who is unreceptive today may be receptive tomorrow. Those who are unreceptive or indifferent can be cultivated. Those with hard hearts can be softened to God. Such changes in receptivity are often referred to as "seasons of the soul." Just as there is a season to plant and a season to harvest, so there are seasons of people's lives when they are "ripe to harvest," or responsive to the Gospel.

What produces seasons of the soul? What makes a person receptive to God? What softens a person who is hardened to the Gospel? There are both supernatural and natural factors that make a receptive-responsive person.

The supernatural factors that make a receptive-responsive person are (1) the conviction of the Holy Spirit whereby a person sees his sin and its result, (2) the influence of the Word of God, (3) the guidance of the Lord that brings a man to understand his condition, and (4) the natural revelation of God in the world.

But there are natural factors that make a person receptive to God. Some of these natural factors are transitions of life that disrupt the normal area of security a person has, such as (1) marriage, (2) the birth of a child, (3) job change such as firing or bankruptcy, (4) sickness, (5) death in the family, or (6) being jailed. Any time a person goes through a social disequilibrium, or culture shock, he becomes a receptive-responsive person.

When a person moves from one home to another he may become receptive to God, especially if he moves far enough away to disrupt family and friendship roots. A person who has been reared Roman Catholic, in another city will attend a Bible-preaching church and become open to its message. This will happen especially if he has a positive relationship to someone in the church. Moving one's home makes a person receptive, also the loss of familiar emotional ties increases his receptivity. The influence of a Bible Christian adds another level of receptivity.

Receptivity must extend to both the messenger and the message. It is possible for a person to reject either the messenger or the message. Jesus warned about this twofold possibility when He told His disciples, "And whoever will not receive you nor hear your words, when you depart from that house or city, shake off the dust from your feet" (Matt. 10:14). The words of that verse translated *receive* and *hear* mean "to approve" and "to give ear." The two possibilities of rejection were (1) the unsaved would reject the messenger, and (2) refuse to listen to the message.

In practice, some received the messenger but rejected the message. The rich young ruler apparently had confidence in Jesus. He addressed Jesus as "Good Master," or literally, "Good Teacher." The word for *good* means "upright, honorable, or acceptable." The rich young ruler seems to have been quite receptive to the Messenger.

As Jesus began answering his questions, the young ruler's

attitude changed. He was not willing to receive the message that required him to part with his riches (19:21-22). He was receptive to the Messenger but he rejected the message.

Today, some fail to hear the message of salvation because they reject the messenger. When Jesus returned to His hometown of Nazareth, He went to the synagogue and began teaching (13:54-57). The people were astonished, literally "struck with amazement," by the wisdom of the message He proclaimed. However, they refused to receive the message because they rejected the Messenger. The word *offended* in verse 57 is the same word rendered "stumbling-block" in Romans 11:9 and 1 Corinthians 1:23. They were impressed by the message of Jesus, but stumbled over the Messenger.

The church should evangelize all its "Jerusalem" by using as many means as possible. But the church should also invest its priority time reaching those who are receptive-responsive people because (1) time is short, (2) resources are limited, (3) it follows the biblical example, and (4) through making disciples it produces greater results.

If a pastor can make only five evangelistic visits during a period of time, it would seem wise that he place priority on visiting those who are receptive and responsive. Why? Because emphasizing receptive-responsive people is (1) trying to be as fruitful as possible for Christ, (2) winning the winnable while they are winnable, before their receptivity cools, (3) growing the church faster and larger, and (4) being a good steward of one's time and resources.

Time and resources are limited. Therefore, there should be a stewardship of these factors in every aspect of life, even evangelism. Jesus Himself clearly taught that evangelistic efforts should reach all (Mark 16:15) but concentrate on those who are receptive and responsive (Matt. 10:14). This principle brought about the turning point in the Apostle Paul's ministry (Acts 13:46).

In light of his stewardship, the Christian must establish priorities for evangelism. He must be interested in reaching all, but he also must determine where his evangelistic efforts are likely to be most productive, and give that area attention. That does not mean he can forget or ignore the rest of the world. It does mean, however, that he should determine which people are likely to be most receptive and responsive to him, then concentrate his efforts on them.

The churches that are growing through evangelism are (1) locating those in their communities who are most receptive to the Gospel, (2) establishing relationships with them, (3) presenting the Gospel to them, and (4) moving those who are less receptive to become more receptive to Christ.

Time is so limited, and resources are scarce. We cannot spend equal time on all the people in the world, trying to reach them for Christ. So first we must evangelize all, using every available means at our disposal. Then, we must give quality time to reach receptive-responsive people. Good stewardship demands that time be invested where it will bring the greatest return for the glory of God. In the area of evangelism, that means targeting receptive-responsive people, and making a concentrated effort to stairstep them toward a decision for Christ.

STEP 67   Follow-up All Visitors
F.R.A.N.GELISM is an evangelistic program with a built-in follow-up. In F.R.A.N.GELISM, we speak of reaching the reachable while they are reachable and winning the winnable while they are winnable. Two key components in this strategy are a program of stairstepping people to Christ and a program of bonding people to the church.

Stairstepping is nothing more than a systematic and natural approach of bringing people to Christ. It allows the Christian to keep the ultimate objective in clear focus and, at the same time, see where the candidate is in the process of evangelism. The unique quality of stairstepping is that it takes the guesswork out of evangelism and provides an objective means of measuring progress.

The entire church's undershepherds team must be aware of the stairstepping goal. They will come in contact with people on different steps. Their aim is to network people into the church and stairstep them to a meaningful decision for Christ.

Barriers must be removed. The unsaved must hear the Gospel often so they will become more receptive to it.

The key to getting people converted and "BONDED" so they continue with Christ and the church is to understand what goes on inside of them before they are saved.

UNDERSTANDING THAT LEADS TO BONDING
Pre-Conversion
Salvation
Post-Conversion

The key to getting started is determining where the prospect is in relationship to God. The evangelist then knows what entry level to make in witnessing to the unchurched. Once a relationship has been made, the process of evangelism is a matter of stairstepping the prospect toward faith in Christ.

Stairstepping is taking a holistic view to the task of evangelism or disciple-making. It includes all that is involved in reaching the unsaved where they are and bringing them to Christ. It is moving people through a process, which is accomplished one step at a time.

The chart on the next page shows the entire process. The initial contact could be made with a person at any level. An unsaved person is not required to begin on the first step. Therefore, stairstepping can begin or end with any of the various steps in the process.

Stairstepping is both supernatural and natural. Many things bring a person to Christ, such as the power of the Gospel, the convicting work of the Holy Spirit, and the drawing of the Father. The power of God that brings salvation resides in the Gospel, not in any human program or humanly devised scheme (Rom. 1:16). Only the Holy Spirit can convict the sinner (John 16:8), and every precaution must be taken to see that no conscious or unconscious attempt is made to replace spiritual conviction with psychological pressure or human manipulation.

The Unchurched

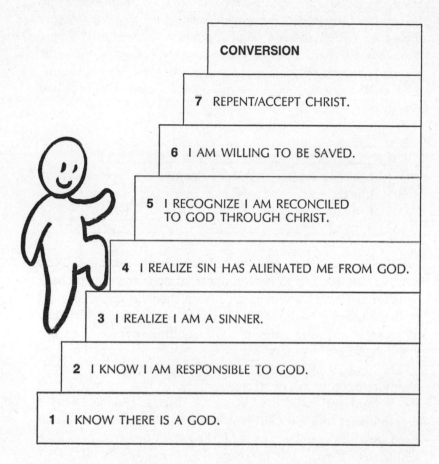

CONVERSION

7 REPENT/ACCEPT CHRIST.

6 I AM WILLING TO BE SAVED.

5 I RECOGNIZE I AM RECONCILED TO GOD THROUGH CHRIST.

4 I REALIZE SIN HAS ALIENATED ME FROM GOD.

3 I REALIZE I AM A SINNER.

2 I KNOW I AM RESPONSIBLE TO GOD.

1 I KNOW THERE IS A GOD.

Regardless of human effort, only God can draw sinners to Himself (6:44).

At the same time, it is neither logical nor biblical to expect an atheist on the first step to make a decision to repent and trust Jesus Christ without taking some intermediate steps in his understanding and acceptance of the person of God. Also, before he can exercise faith in Christ, he must understand the provision Christ has made for his redemption (Heb. 11:6).

In evangelism, the decision to trust Jesus Christ by faith is preceded by many other decisions. Some of those decisions may be subconscious, or they may come so early in life that the person has forgotten that he made them, but they must nevertheless be made. Unsaved people do not repent and trust Christ until they see their need and understand the Gospel. Looking at the stairstepping process, it is obvious that each step is dependent on the one before it. Stairstepping is natural to effective evangelism.

EVANGELISM LIFE CYCLE CHART				
Event	Process	Event	Process	Event
Initial Contact	Stair- stepping	New Birth	Spiritual Growth	Rapture Death

Churches are too often like flow-through tea bags. New members are allowed to flow in the front door and out the back with little effective effort made to stop them. A church should be like a sponge, taking in all it can find, and keeping all it gets. That is where the principle of bonding comes into the F.R.A.N.GELISM program.

The process of bonding newcomers to the church is commonly referred to as post-evangelism, but it is actually a part of the biblical and holistic processes of disciple-making. After a person comes to know Christ, it is imperative to get him assimilated into the church. The Bible knows nothing of free-lance Christians. Throughout the New Testament, those who were saved became active members of an existing local church, or local churches were formed, and they became active in them.

A holistic approach to evangelism requires that provision be made for the new Christian's normal growth and development. That normal growth and development requires that the new Christian become settled in, or bonded to, a local church. That is where he will be brought under the ministry of the Word of God that will result in spiritual growth (1 Peter 2:2), victory over sin (Ps. 119:9-11), answered prayer (John 15:7), and strengthened faith (Rom. 10:17). The local church is also where the new Christian will be able to grow through fellowship with other Christians (Heb. 10:25).

When the local church fails in the bonding process, and the new Christian stops attending church regularly (or is out of the church completely), the growth and development process is handicapped.

Bonding is essential to the task of closing the back door of the church. Nothing is more frustrating than spending time and effort to win people to Christ and then watching them become unfaithful, join another local church, or drop out of church completely. But that is exactly what happens when the task of bonding is not taken seriously. New Christians drift from one Sunday School class to another, and from one social group to another, trying to find a place where they are made to feel like a vital and needed part of the church. If such a place is not found, they become discouraged and stop searching. In time, they either become casual church members, move to another church, or just drop out of church.

Bonding is a biblical pattern. The first church, the one started in Jerusalem on the Day of Pentecost, grew more rapidly than any church since that time. Yet those early Christians were able to keep the back door effectively closed. Why? The reason is simple. New Christians were bonded to the church. Their felt needs were met by the church (Acts 2:44), and they were made to feel a part of the church family (v. 42). Those who were already members were willing and anxious to make room for the newcomers (v. 47).

It is often assumed that new Christians and new members are bonded to the church when they join. In practice, nothing could be farther from the truth. If such an assumption is made, the back door will always swing wide. The key to the bonding process is NOT church membership but church ownership. Newcomers are bonded to the church only when they begin to think of the church in terms of "my church," and that only happens when they begin to feel like a vital part of the church as a whole or some group or organization within the church.

THE LAW OF SEVEN TOUCHES
F.R.A.N.GELISM follow-up

STEP 68 Touch One—Phone Call
When someone visits the church on a Sunday morning (usually the most common time for a person to make a first visit to a new church), they should be immediately followed up in accordance with the laws of the three hearings and seven touches.

The first of these seven contacts or touches is Sunday afternoon. The pastor, teacher, or an outreach worker should phone the visitor and thank him for his attendance. The phone call should establish three things. First, the caller should offer spiritual help to the visitor and his family. Second, he will want to mention the special "Friendship Packet" the church has prepared for them and that someone would like to deliver the packet to their home. Third, the visitor should be told someone from the church will phone for an appointment to bring the packet to the home. It is important that the unchurched realize that someone from the church will not "drop in" unannounced.

STEP 69 Touch Two—A Letter
The next of the seven touches occurs Sunday evening. The pastor or Sunday School teacher should write a letter covering much of what he said during the phone call. This could be a standard form letter that comes off a home computer which goes out to visitors, but if so, each letter should be personalized to the recipient.

STEP 70 Touch Three—The Secretary's Phone Call
The secretary phones to make an appointment for someone from the church to visit the prospect and deliver the Friendship Packet. Suggest a time for the visit to their home during the phone call. As soon as an appointment is made, the secretary will send a follow-up letter confirming the time. Because it is important to win the winnable while they are winnable and reach the reachable while they are reachable, many churches find Tuesday evening a good time for this second phone call.

When suggesting a time, be approximate so as to give you liberty to stay longer or leave earlier on other visits you may make that evening. You might suggest you could drop by around 7 P.M. on Wednesday evening.

STEP 71 Fourth Touch—Appointment Letter

After the Tuesday evening phone call, write a letter to the prospect confirming the time of the visit. (Even though some letters arrive after the visit because of delays in postal service, it is part of the accumulative effect of F.R.A.N.GELISM Follow-up.) Again express your willingness to help them spiritually and assure them they are welcome to visit the church services as often as they can.

STEP 72 Fifth Touch—The Visit

On Wednesday or Thursday evening, someone from the church or the Sunday School class in which they would be involved should visit them. Ideally, this should be the teacher, but if there are a number of people to help, it is better that another class officer or member make the visit rather than putting it off several weeks until the teacher can make the call.

The primary reason for visiting the home is to present Jesus Christ to the person. Beyond this, the pastor/teacher should be alert to the need in the home and apply the Gospel to any problems that are brought up by the unchurched.

During this visit, the teacher should tell the prospect about the class and how they could fit into the class. He will also want to be familiar with the rest of the church program that might be of interest to others in the family, i.e., children's and youth ministries.

STEP 73 Sixth Touch—Follow-Up Letter

The pastor/teacher should immediately take the time to write a letter to the prospect outlining the next spiritual step he should take. After the visit, the pastor/teacher should know if the person needs to accept Christ, rededicate himself, join the church, or whatever. This letter should clearly outline what is expected. The letter should also thank him for letting the pastor/teacher visit and again extend the invitation to visit the appropriate Sunday School class that Sunday.

STEP 74 Seventh Touch—The Saturday Night Friendly Phone Call

An informal follow-up with a phone call on Saturday inviting the prospect to the Sunday School class or service the next day provides the finishing touches to a week of following up a receptive-responsive person. By the end of the week, the casual visitor has met several people from the church and recognizes the church is interested in him. Unless there is some particular reason why he cannot, it is very likely the visitor will return to the church where he knows he is welcome and accepted.

STEP 75 Networking People to the Church

The success of F.R.A.N.GELISM is networking people to the Gospel. It begins with friendship, not confrontation. After a relationship is established, the person is confronted with his need to accept Jesus Christ (John 14:6).

STEP 76 Follow-up Leads to Bonding

It is imperative that the church bond new members to a primary group within the church as soon as possible. Research shows that to keep a new believer in the church, he must become a part of a social group (class or cell), or make a relationship to someone in the church within two weeks or he will probably drop out of the church. If the new believer has a friend in the church, he will probably remain faithful. Therefore, networking or "bonding" new believers to a cell, or primary group, is imperative if the church is to grow.

New Christians and new church members are not automatically bonded to a church when they join the church. Existing groups within the church do not automatically reach out to draw in newcomers and make them feel a part of the group and/or the church body. Even those newcomers who seek out, find, and join a group (cell) where they think they will fit, often continue to feel like outsiders.

Actually, if within two weeks new members have not made a friendship relationship in the church or joined a group, they will probably not stay within the church. They will become discouraged, move to another church, or drop out of church altogether.

Something must be done to close the back door of the church. Newcomers must be bonded to the church, and it is the responsibility of the church to provide the glue for that bonding.

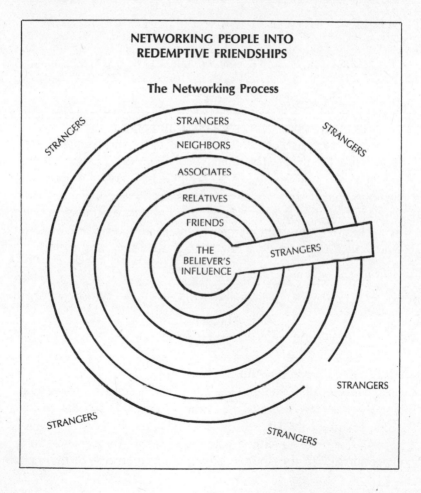

9

THE ADULT BIBLE CLASS

In recent years, there has been a noticeable trend in Sunday School from an emphasis on children to an emphasis on adults. Prior to 1971, the average American Sunday School was filled with about 38 percent adults. Today, that figure has risen to 51 percent. This is a dramatic demographical shift in the Sunday School population that should affect the total program. Don't think of Sunday School as a children's program. It has become an adult place because over half those attending Sunday School today are adults.

SUNDAY SCHOOL
THE ADULT PLACE

STEP 77 Focus on Adults
More specifically, the growing edge in the Sunday School during the past few years is the Young Adult Class, ages 18-35. This is perhaps the largest "mission field" for the Sunday School today. There are 50 million young couples in America who must be reached with the Gospel. But it can also be one of the most

demanding of groups to reach. This is the "Now Generation" that likes instant gratification. Also, they tend to be somewhat hedonistic, making decisions on the basis of what is in it for them.

On July 23, 1987, *The Minneapolis Tribune* printed an article entitled, "Boomers Return to Church" noting that many in the church realized they lost a generation and are now surprised to see the Baby Boomers (now ages 18-40) return to the church.

Why? A recent survey showed those ages 18-35 are perhaps among the most receptive-responsive people in our ministry. This is why they represent the fastest-growing age-group in the Sunday School. Since the receptive-responsive are also those who are marked by "the seasons of the soul," we should note the transitions they are undergoing.

In view of the tremendous number of choices and transitions facing young adults, no wonder they are a fruitful field for soul winning and church recruitment.

TRANSITION FOR AGES 18–35
1 Choosing a college.
2 Choosing a major.
3 Choosing courses.
4 Choosing roommates, new friends.
5 Adjusting to a new city/environment.
6 Re-choosing a major/college/roommate, etc.
7 Choosing a career after college.
8 Choosing a new city/apartment/ friends/etc. after college.
9 Choosing a life partner.
10 Re-choosing a job/city/friends/life partner/etc.

STEP 78 Begin New Adult Classes
To effectively reach adults, we must create classes in structure

OPEN CLASSES PSYCHOGRAPHICS	AGE-GRADE CLASSES DEMOGRAPHICS
Open to all adults, regardless of age, sex, or marital status.	Assigns adults to a class with others who have similar age, sex, and marital status.
Classes tend to center around a psychological need, drive, or personality. They become homogeneous units or cells which are the basis for church growth.	No adult in the Sunday School is overlooked because there is a class for every age, sex, and marital status.
High degree of loyalty because their needs are met.	A class for everyone and everyone in a class.
Whereas age-graded classes for adults eventually run out of divisions, the number of open classes is endless.	Loyalty by all to the whole system because of a comprehensive ministry to all.

for adults (age-graded classes). But we must also create open classes. The structure is like the skeleton which gives strength to the body. But the open class is like the heart which gives feeling to the body. While we must organize adult classes according to the principles of age-grading to effect a structure which best meets the unique needs of adults at various times during their maturing, we must not forget the auditorium Bible class which is open to all.

In starting new Bible classes, think psychographically rather than demographically. Psychographically is considering the psychological needs of people that draw a group together.

These may be classes for the single adults, single again (divorced persons), single parents, young married couples, expecting couples, young couples, business and professional women, senior saints, teacher training, new members, widows, the deaf, and mentally retarded. Next consider open Bible classes which are open to all ages, both sexes, and the married or single. These classes complement the traditional auditorium Bible class, also called the pastor's Bible class.

The structured classes are adult age-graded classes. This may be a class for the men ages 25 to 29 or a class for couples ages 30 to 39. Structured classes make sure that no one age-group/need is overlooked in the church.

STEP 79 Give Priority to Shepherding a Class
The teacher must give the class a high spiritual priority, putting nothing else in the church before his commitment to that class. If the class is not the most important ministry of the church so far as the teacher is concerned, it is doubtful he will be very successful in attracting others to become involved in class projects.

STEP 80 Give Adult Classes Priority in Classroom Selection
Have a room that can be used each week. A room will help the new class develop a sense of unique identity much faster than if the class is constantly moved from place to place each week.

Do not do anything less for children. However, put your classroom strategy on reaching adults. Poor facilities become a barrier to attracting adults.

STEP 81 Decorate the Room for Adults
Decorate the room according to the needs and interests of members. An attractive room will help give the room a personality rather than just bare walls. Also, it will lead to a greater degree of involvement from the class members during the times spent together in the room. Decorating the room could possibly be the first class project done together.

It is estimated that 70 to 80 percent of the educational budget is invested on children in Sunday School, but the children are only about 38 percent of the Sunday School. To correct this imbalance, it is important that we do not spend less on the children. Rather, it is time to begin spending more on adults.

STEP 82 Hold Class Prayer Meetings

Hold regular prayer meetings apart from Sunday morning. As class members meet to pray for each other and the needs of the class, they will want to become more involved in using their class to meet the needs of others.

For many years, the Steadfast Bible Class in my church had a group of approximately eight men who met every Saturday morning for prayer and breakfast. This class of over 100 is 31 years old at the writing of this book and is responsible for supporting missionaries on the field and sending some of its members into the pastorate.

STEP 83 Have Class Projects

Plan class projects for those who want to get involved physically in the ministry. For every Mary who wants to sit at the feet of Jesus, there is a Martha who wants to do something (Luke 10:38-42). When classes work together, they grow together. In most churches and communities, there is always an abundance of things an adult Bible class could do as a class project.

SUGGESTED PROJECTS
1 Paint, install carpet, drapes, lamps, etc.
2 Install sink for coffee and refreshments.
3 Put out a class newsletter.
4 Purchase or paint furniture.
5 Install screen and overhead.
6 Work on church mailing.
7 Repair home for elderly members.
8 Write missionaries and report back.
9 Manual jobs around the church.
10 Care for sick, shut-in, etc.

STEP 84   Have Class Names

Choose a class name. Over the years, it seems that giving names to Sunday School classes has gone full cycle. Fifty years ago and beyond, all adult classes had names. Then, generic titles were given such as men's class, ages 30-35. Now names are coming back into popularity because they give identity and/or feeling to a class. With the name, you will want to adopt a class logo and motto. Just as these are used in business to help potential customers readily identify a product or service, so they will help class members to identify with the class.

Bill Newton took the fourth-grade boys class at the Thomas Road Baptist Church, Lynchburg, Virginia and called it "The Treehouse Gang." A massive cardboard tree with a door was used at the entrance of the room. Two more large trees, reaching from floor to ceiling, covered the inside walls. Later, a stockade was put in the hall surrounding the doors. Bill Newton started his class in September. His goal was to average 54 boys before the year was out. With enthusiasm, ingenuity, and determination, Newton pushed the average attendance to 94.

The Indianapolis Baptist Temple had an unusual logo and motto for its 25th anniversary in 1975. A huge silver seal hung all year in the auditorium with the motto, "The 25th Year of Redemption." Under the motto was their goal, "2,500 Souls

SUGGESTED NAMES FOR ADULT CLASSES
The Faith-Way Class
The Pioneers
The Bible Seekers Class
The Bible Lovers Class
The Genesis Class (newly married)
The Rebuilders (single parents)
The Single Vision Class (singles)
The New Life Class (recent converts)
The Overcomers
The Sonship Class

Won to Christ in 1975." The entire seal was their logo. They had it fashioned into small silver seals which they affixed to envelopes and letterheads. It was also printed on all the literature of the church.

STEP 85   Begin a Class Newsletter

With the availability of a photocopier or instant print service, it is possible to make copies of a one-page newsletter inexpensively. Every class should have a written communication to its members. Even a very small class could produce a class newsletter regularly during a special attendance building campaign.

The junior class at the Crestwicke Baptist Church, Ontario distributes an eight-page paper, *The Roadrunner*, to every junior. Since it is a large class, the teachers spend time writing articles about juniors who have recently committed their lives to Jesus Christ. The paper also includes crossword puzzles, homework, stories, and news about the attendance campaign. The attendance motto and logo are also printed there, reminding the kids of their attendance goal.

A newsletter is not hard to prepare. If you have never issued one, simply write a one-page letter giving the news of the class. Then type the letter in two columns to make it look like a newspaper, and put a headline across the top. Fill the newspaper with the names of students, their accomplishments, and what you expect to do for God. In preparing your newspaper, you will want to include many of the following items:

STEP 86   Include Statistics

You will want to include class statistics about the class offerings, attendance, new members, and projects.

STEP 87   Include Names of Visitors in Newsletters

Publishing the names of visitors to the class in the newsletter will help class members identify and call newer members by name. This will demonstrate to visitors they are viewed as more than just statistics.

STEP 88   Include Events and Projects in the Newsletter
Use the newsletter to advertise upcoming events and projects of interest to the class.

STEP 89   Include a Message from the Teacher in the
Newsletter
You may also want to include a brief devotional message from the teacher. It is at this place the teacher will give direction to the class. The newsletter will help him to pastor his flock corporately.

STEP 90   Get Officers for Adult Classes
You will want to elect class officers/leaders to give members a greater degree of involvement in the way their class is conducted. A class could also elect a class president/leader who might be responsible for leading meetings of the class and coordinating the activities of the other class officers/leaders. Group leaders could also be elected with responsibilities in the areas of outreach, absentee follow-up, fellowship, and hospitality. A class should also have a secretary to keep records and a treasurer to count the money. Many classes are combining these responsibilities into one person and calling him/her a receptionist or a host/hostess who relates to people while a secretary/treasurer relates to figures.

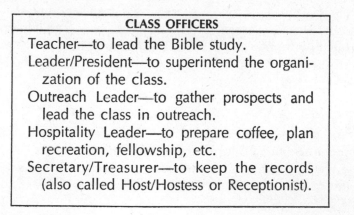

CLASS OFFICERS
Teacher—to lead the Bible study.
Leader/President—to superintend the organization of the class.
Outreach Leader—to gather prospects and lead the class in outreach.
Hospitality Leader—to prepare coffee, plan recreation, fellowship, etc.
Secretary/Treasurer—to keep the records (also called Host/Hostess or Receptionist).

STEP 91 Install a Coffeepot for Fellowship

You will also want to invest in a coffeepot for your class. The coffeepot has come to symbolize fellowship in adult Bible classes today. They are not abandoning Bible study for coffee, nor is coffee a gimmick to attract people to the class. Rather, leaders are combining their Bible study with fellowship. People are not attracted to the class simply because there are refreshments available. They come because of the opportunity to have fellowship with friends. The key to growing classes is Bible study with fellowship. Not Bible teaching with fellowship, nor Bible explanation with fellowship. *BIBLE STUDY* is an attitude of involvement by all in discussion. Openness to personal interaction with the Bible is stimulated by fellowship around a cup of coffee.

STEP 92 Get a Receptionist

Have a receptionist to meet people as they arrive in class. Historically, this task was done by a class secretary, but the name receptionist suggests a people person. Some classes accomplish this task by assigning hosts and hostesses for their class each week.

The receptionist will take roll, the offering, and distribute any printed announcements or lesson helps. A good hostess can offer a personal greeting to all who attend.

STEP 93 Name Tags Help Friendship

Prepare name tags for everyone, class members and visitors. Name tags put everyone on a first name basis. The informality created by name tags will help class members involve visitors in their discussions and make visitors and newer class members feel like a part of the group.

STEP 94 Adult Classes Bond New Members

Adult classes are the glue that keeps people from drifting through the church. Beginning new adult Bible classes will help the church keep more of the adults it is reaching through its ministry. Also, it will be a base of outreach to other adults in the community.

How important is the adult Bible class in the process of bonding people to the church? Research shows that to keep a new believer in the church, he must become a part of a social group (class or cell), or make a relationship to someone in the church within two weeks or he will probably drop out of the church.

ADULT CLASSES ARE THE GLUE THAT BONDS NEW MEMBERS TO A CHURCH¹

GROUPS KEEP NEW CONVERTS/MEMBERS IN THE CHURCH
Why adult classes do not incorporate new members

STEP 95 Inbreeding Prohibits Outreach
Why is it then that some adult classes do not incorporate new members into their group? One reason may be that the class has become inbred. Christians only fellowship with Christians. When cattle inbreed they produce runts or go sterile. When Christians just fellowship with other Christians their classes become sterile. Attempting to avoid this problem is one reason

why some promote the "divide and multiply" approach to Sunday School growth. Another way is to recruit "seed members" to go and begin a new class. Constantly beginning new classes will break inbreeding. When Christians only have fellowship with other Christians, it will dry up their evangelistic fervor. Unconsciously, they cut outsiders out of their group, thus preventing any possibility for growth.

Most primary groups are naturally resistant to outsiders. If this natural tendency is not neutralized by a conscious effort to welcome newcomers, the group will unintentionally and usually unknowingly become a private club. Paul warned the church in Rome against this very danger (Rom. 15:7; 16:2).

STEP 96 Sociological Tissue Rejection Kills Outreach

A second reason why some adult classes do not incorporate new members has been called by C. Peter Wagner, "sociological tissue rejection." This means people of one class or culture do not "fit" into the lifestyle of the class because it is different from them. If the men of an adult Bible class are down-home boys who talk about pickup trucks, dirt track racing, and redeye gravy, it is unlikely a prospect who is classified as a preppy would have much in common because he likes hot air balloons, quiche, and wears button-down collars. When these two cultures clash in an adult Bible class, the yuppy usually drops out because of "sociological tissue rejection." Just as some organ transplants do not mesh, so some people do not become comfortable in certain Sunday School classes. To some extent, this is a natural tendency in all groups because they tend to be homogeneous. If a class is going to grow, it needs to make a conscious effort to reach out to others who are like them.

Perhaps this explains why some people do not choose a church simply because it is affiliated with a particular denomination or close to their home. In a survey conducted among members of Presbyterian churches in a large American city, it was learned two out of three Presbyterians pass a church to get to their Presbyterian church. A similar survey conducted by Southern Baptists concluded that approximately two out of three

Southern Baptists pass a Baptist church to get to the Baptist church they choose to attend.

STEP 97   Range Wars Kill Outreach

A third reason why some adult classes fail to incorporate new members is seen in the traditional conflict between the pioneers versus the land rights of settlers. Just as the pioneering cowboys had range wars when settlers put up barbed wire, so some Christians keep out those who want to pioneer for Christ. Those who begin the class often have a different commitment than those who join the class at some later date. The pioneers want to reach out and win new members to Christ. Sometimes those who move their membership into the church are "settlers." They want to just settle down in their class. Those who help plant new churches are pioneers. This difference, if not recognized and dealt with, could lead to internal conflict which will hinder the outreach of the class.

HOW TO KEEP ADULT CLASSES GROWING

STEP 98   Be Number Conscious

Few classes will ever grow if they do not have a growth attitude. This attitude is best expressed in numerical goals, or numerical measurement. Though some leaders may object to being number-oriented in the ministry, emphasis on numbers is biblical. God numbered things because number comparison reflects growth. God loves growth. He caused living things to grow. Notice the things in the Bible that are numbered: the 7 days of Creation, the 12 tribes of Israel, the 12 disciples, the 70 sent out, the 144,000 among other groups. God even called one of the books in Scripture Numbers.

The early Jerusalem church was measured by numerical growth. This one church had 120 in the Upper Room (Acts 1:15), 3,000 were added to them (2:41), 5,000 men were counted (4:4), then the church multiplied (6:1), and then multiplied greatly (v. 7), and finally a number of churches were spun off and the churches multiplied (9:31).

As one pastor put it so well, "We count people because people count!"

Some people seem to think there must be a conflict between quality and quantity in the ministry, i.e., that you can't have one without rejecting the other. But quality and quantity can and should go together in every ministry. That was certainly the case in the Book of Acts where a quality ministry experienced rapid and sustained growth.

There are several reasons why every small adult class should want to grow. First, growth is biblical. The churches of the New Testament grew unless there was a problem with sin in the church. Second, a class should grow because of the biblical mandate of evangelism (Matt. 28:19-20). Evangelizing classes are growing classes. Third, the larger the class, the more likely there will be class members with spiritual gifts (1 Cor. 7:7) who can minister to the total needs of other class members, hence, "edifying . . . itself" (Eph. 4:11-16). Fourth, some members are more comfortable in a large growing class because they draw less attention and they are less likely to be called on, yet they feel part of a dynamic body. And fifth, the large growing class usually has an effective teacher who can effectively communicate the Word of God to a larger group of people. Many choose a large class because they learn more and experience broadly the Word of God.

There is nothing inherently wrong with a large adult Bible class. Nor is there anything wrong with a small class. Both have their contribution, and those in one should be tolerant of the other. As we continue to reach people with the Gospel, we should grow spiritually as we see our class grow both internally and/or externally.

STEP 99   Be Willing to Start New Classes

There must be a willingness to start new groups (classes, departments, service groups, new churches, etc.). Most of the new growth in the church will come as a result of beginning new groups rather than from the older established classes.

There are two basic reasons for the creation of new classes.

One, all newcomers may not be able to find a place of involvement in an existing class. If this is the case, the creation of new classes may be necessary to provide a suitable place for them.

Every Christian is a new creation in Christ (2 Cor. 5:17), and each is created differently (1 Cor. 12:29-30). Each has different needs, different natural abilities, different spiritual gifts, and different burdens for ministry. Newcomers should be expected to fit into classes for which they are suited.

Christian unity does not require uniformity. The local church is a body of Christ (v. 27), but a body is made up of many different parts (v. 12), and God intends that a place should be provided for each member to fit and function (vv. 13-25).

The second reason for creating new classes is that existing classes are usually saturated. Many groups cannot effectively accommodate additional members. A ball team, church choir, or Sunday School class with limited seating space are prime examples.

There are two methods of creating new classes. One is through division and the other is by multiplication. Division involves splitting an existing class into two classes. This often meets strong resistance. Since classes are the glue that holds the church together, such forced division can be destructive.

Multiplication of cells is accomplished by recruiting individuals to form a nucleus of a new class. This method is far more safe because it does not apply undue outside pressure. A small number of people are asked to serve as "seed members" or a nucleus for the new class. The class develops around that seed group. Once the new class is established, the seed group may remain with the new class or return to their original class.

STEP 100 New Members Join a Class When Joining the Church

New members should be automatically incorporated into the adult classes when they join the church. The Frank Adams family joined a Baptist church in Montgomery, Alabama. When the pastor found out that Frank had been an usher in the previous church where his family attended, he was recruited into the job.

The ushers became Frank's new primary group and the Adams family was immediately bonded to the new church.

The Manuel Rodriguez family walked forward to join a church in northern Indiana. They had never been active in a church. Manuel was recruited to drive a Sunday School bus. He found fellowship with the other bus workers and began growing in Christ through his service. Manuel never missed a Sunday because he was bonded to the church.

In the winter of 1984, I visited First Baptist Church, Euliss, Texas, where Dr. James Draper is pastor. That evening five people walked forward to join the church. There were three women and two men; their ages ranged between 20 and 40. As Dr. Draper called each name of the new members to introduce them to the church, the pastor told them what Sunday School class they would be attending. Dr. Draper then called the name of the teacher who came forward and stood next to the new members. Then he asked other class members to come and meet their new members. The front of the auditorium was filled with several from each Sunday School class who met the new members.

Another church introduces the people or a group who graduate from the membership class to the church. As people are introduced and voted into fellowship, the congregation is advised what adult Bible class they will attend and what task each has in the church. This is along with information on their conversion, baptism, etc.

STEP 101   Teachers Are Pastor/Evangelists

The class will keep growing when the teacher remembers he has the task of a pastor/evangelist. As a pastor he is a shepherd; as an evangelist, he is a soul-winner. Everything the pastor is in the life of the church, the Sunday School teacher should be in the life of the class. When the total church is growing, so should the class, and vice versa.

Active involvement in the local church is essential to the proper growth and development of Christians. Peter wrote, "As newborn babes, desire the pure milk of the Word, that you may grow thereby" (1 Peter 2:2). Spiritual growth, like physical growth, requires proper feeding, and God has provided for feeding through the ministry of the local church. He has given gifted individuals to the church for the purpose of perfecting or maturing the saints (Eph. 4:11-12), and these gifted individuals exercise their ministry in local assemblies or flocks (1 Peter 5:2-3).

Since the local church is the God-ordained center for growth, active involvement in the local church is essential to proper and normal development. The unsaved must not only be brought to Christ, but be drawn into the local church as well.

RECOGNIZE THE NATURE OF GROUPS

STEP 102   Small Classes Provide Intimacy
The character of a group will change as it grows. A leader must know the nature of groups (classes, departments, or cells), what a group will do for the total church, and what a group will do for the individual. A small group of 8 to 12 members will provide an intimate relationship between members and will provoke intense loyalty on the part of the members to the class. Small Sunday School classes of long-term duration such as a ladies' or men's Bible class will have a deeper degree of loyalty than larger classes or short-term classes. A leader should know the contribution of a class according to its size and that not every class will provide the same ministry to all members. Some will seek out small classes because they desire intimacy, while others will seek out large classes because of the quality of instruction. Never try to force every class into the same mold (uniformity), nor every person into the same type of class.

STEP 103   Medium Classes Provide Fellowship
A larger group/class of 13 to 30 members is characterized by fellowship. This medium-sized class cannot have the intimacy of small classes because of the multiplied number of relationships. As the class grows in size, the relationships become less intense and the members' loyalty becomes less intense.

STEP 104 Large Classes Have Zones of Fellowship
A group of 30 to 100 members will tend to form fellowship zones. Group members may not know everyone in the group, but they will group themselves with whom they tend to fellowship within the larger group. People are creatures of habit and they will sit in the same area each week and talk to the same people. They will zone themselves; the leader never has to do this.

STEP 105 Super Classes Need Proclamation Explanation
When a group grows above 100, the very size of the group virtually dictates the teacher must assume the role of a proclaimer or lecturer. Some church growth authorities call this celebration. I teach a pastor's Bible class of approximately 2,000 in attendance. I realize we do not have intimacy and there is not a deep level of fellowship within the group. However, there are some zones of fellowship, because the same people tend to sit in the same areas each week and speak to those around them. I explain/proclaim the Word of God. There are many who would rather be in a large class than a smaller, intimate class. The large class meets their needs. At the same time we have many small classes for those who choose intimacy, fellowship, and discussion.

This large class also has another function. It is a conduit for visitors to find their way to a smaller class in the church where they can have intimacy or fellowship. They attend my class until they find a class where they are comfortable. Some have called the large class the handshake to the church.

HOW LARGE CAN A CELL BE S-T-R-E-T-C-H-E-D?

There are at least two answers to the question as to how large a cell can be s-t-r-e-t-c-h-e-d. Lyle Schaller suggests a group can be stretched to include 40 members. The author believes a cell can be stretched farther, to include up to 59 members. I took a number of students to Wheaton, Illinois to do sociograms on a random selection of attenders at three churches. The first church had 100, the second 300, and the third averaged 1,200 in attendance. We found the average attender knew 59.7 people by name in each congregation. Hence, the average church member knows the name of only about 59 of his fellow members. Some could name only 3 or 4 in their congregation while others could name all 200. Being able to recognize others may lead to a false view of church size, when it is said, "I wouldn't want to attend a large church. I wouldn't know everyone." Remember, the purpose of a church is not to know other people, it is to carry out the Great Commission.

PRACTICAL STEPS TO GROW THE SUNDAY SCHOOL CLASS

STEP 106   Pray for Growth

The first practical step in growing a Sunday School class is to pray! God has promised to answer our requests, "And whatever you ask in My name, that I will do, that the Father may be glorified in the Son" (John 14:13).

STEP 107   Pray for Specific Goals

As you intercede for your class, pray for your attendance goals. Get your class members to join you in praying for the class attendance goals.

A junior boys class that averaged 12 in attendance at the Forest Hills Baptist Church, Decatur, Georgia set a goal of 25 in Sunday School. They wanted to double their average attendance. The teacher asked each boy to kneel and pray publicly during the Sunday School class for 25 to attend. Then the teacher had each boy promise to contact his buddies before Monday evening to get them committed to attend Sunday School. On Monday the teacher phoned each boy to determine the attendance next Sunday. None of the boys had invited a friend. Then he phoned Tuesday, Wednesday, and Thursday nights, and determined they wouldn't reach their goal. Only two or three had visitors coming. The teacher drove his truck to see each on Saturday and took each boy to invite his buddies to Sunday School the next day. They even went to the local movie house and invited every junior boy in line for the Saturday matinee to Sunday School the following day.

The teacher wondered if they would reach their goal of 25 boys. He counted every boy as he entered the little room. When 10 A.M. arrived they had only 19 present. But visitors kept coming. The boys cheered as they reached their goal of 25, and the visitors kept coming. Soon they were sitting two to a chair and standing in the row. When the teacher finally counted all the heads, there were 50 present.

"I can't teach. There are too many in the room," the teacher said apologetically.

"It's my fault, blame me," one boy in the class confessed. "Last week when we all prayed for a goal of 25," he added, "I asked God for 50."

God honors the prayer of junior boys who ask in faith. And God honors the visitation work of teachers. God blesses faith and works (James 2:17-20).

STEP 108 Pray for Converts

As you pray, ask God for individuals to be saved and bonded to the class. As a result of individual and corporate prayer, you can have more new converts as you reach out evangelistically.

PRAYER GOALS FOR INTERNAL GROWTH
1 That pupils will be enlightened to understand the Scriptures.
2 That Christ may indwell and shine from hearts (Eph. 3:17).
3 That the Holy Spirit would fill pupils (Eph. 5:18).
4 That you would teach with power.
5 That all may grow in grace.

STEP 109 *Pray for Internal Spiritual Growth*

Pray for the spiritual growth of yourself as a teacher and the members of your class. Remember, there is a relationship between the spiritual growth of the class and its numerical growth.

STEP 110 *Quality or Quantity, You Get What You Work For*

God hears and answers the prayers of those who ask for their ministry to be enlarged, but prayer *alone* cannot build a Sunday School. The Law of the Division of Labor has two sections. First, *God will not do what He has commanded us to do.* We are to reach people (Deut. 31:12). Classes grow when teachers are busy visiting, phoning, mailing, and praying all week. But, second, *you can't do what God alone can do.* Only God can work in the heart to convict, draw, convert, and transform a person into the likeness of Jesus Christ. Certain tasks are assigned to us and other tasks are reserved for God. But "we are God's fellow workers" (1 Cor. 3:9). Therefore, you can't build a Sunday School class on prayer alone, and you can't grow a Sunday School class without prayer. As mentioned earlier, faith and work must be combined for the blessing of God.

STEP 111 *Know Your Base*

Before deciding how large you want to build your class, you need to know your present average attendance. Before setting an attendance goal, first determine your base. Your base is the average weekly Sunday School attendance. A base is not measured during the spring when attendance is high, nor during the summer when attendance is down. Add all the weeks into a total and divide by the number of Sundays. Your base is a realistic figure on which you plan growth and make calculations for outreach.

With the notable exception of Southern Baptist churches who build their growth around their enrollment statistics, Sunday Schools calculate growth on their base. (The spiral growth plan of the Southern Baptist Convention is an excellent plan but is difficult to use in churches that do not emphasize enrollment.)

STEP 112   Feed the Flock

Be sure you are "feeding the flock." Quality in your Sunday School teaching is the basis for quantity. However, you can't grow a Sunday School class numerically on quality education, and you can't grow a Sunday School class without quality education. Quality does not automatically insure quantity and vice versa. What a Sunday School leader emphasizes is usually what he gets.

STEP 113   Set Attendance Goals

Usually, a class will not grow unless there is an aim to grow. First, set a long-range attendance goal. Next, set a yearly goal. A goal will keep vision lifted and a challenge before the people. Then set a goal for a high day in the spring or fall.

Usually, one overall attendance goal will not stir all the people in your class. That is why it is advisable to set multiple goals during a Sunday School campaign. This gets several things working for you. Each of several specific goals will challenge the specific need to which it is tied, and will bring about a specific result. Many goals will create momentum and excitement in the church.

The following may be achieved during a Sunday School campaign: (1) an all-time attendance record, (2) the highest average attendance for the spring or fall, (3) the highest average attendance for the year, (4) enrollment goals, (5) departmental goals, (6) highest average attendance for all the buses, (7) highest attendance for an individual bus route, (8) greatest number of visitors, (9) the number of visits made by a worker, (10) the greatest number of phone calls made, (11) a goal for the greatest number of postcards written.

Management by goals. How can a Sunday School superintendent motivate the teachers to carry out the Great Commission? The superintendent should discuss goals with the teachers individually and corporately in a teachers' meeting. Ask each teacher to set class goals. This should provide internal motivation for each teacher because it was a personal goal, and external motivation because the goals for each class should be public.

STEP 114   Set Output Goals

Now that goals have been discussed, they need to be refined. Among the goals you set, you will need some output goals. These are the "bottom line" of expected results. In computer terminology, "output" is the result of what you put in the computer. If your class base is 15, set an attendance output goal of 30. This means you want the class to double during the campaign. When output goals are established, go to the next refinement, input goals.

OUTPUT GOALS
Attendance Goals
Offering Goals
Enrollment/membership Goals
Baptism/conversion Goals

STEP 115   Set Input Goals

The second type of goals you need to set are input goals. These are steps that need to be taken to reach a goal. Just as we must recognize certain causes lead to effects, so input goals include the things you need to do to reach your output goals.

INPUT GOALS
A list of prospects.
The number of visits to make.
The number of phone calls to make.
The number of letters to mail.
The number of people who will pray.

One type of input goal is finding and making a list of new prospects. In order for your class to double, attempt to formulate a list of twice as many prospects as your average attendance. When you reach your input goal of twice as many prospects, you have a basis to expect the output goal, i.e., the class doubles. This means that if each member suggests two names of friends he will bring to church, the class has reached its input goal. If there are 30 in the class, get 60 names on your prospect list. Success in input goals gives the class a sense of success. This will lead to confidence as they pursue output goals.

An adult class of 50 members at the Berean Baptist Church, Salem, Virginia distributed blank cards to members and asked each to submit names of friends he or she would like to see in the class. After two weeks of listing names, the goal still was not reached. Therefore, three ladies were delegated to phone members of the class soliciting names and addresses of prospects. They worked until 100 new names were gathered. They had success in their input goal, then they were excited about contacting prospects. The class had 127 visitors.

STEP 116   Educate to Attendance Goals
Be sure to educate your people to the attendance goals. If you set a goal of 30 in attendance, prepare several posters that have the goal of 30. Saturate your pupils with the goal.

Goal-setting works. A junior class teacher in the Florence, South Carolina Baptist Temple hung a large sheet of paper from one wall to another, then had each of the 26 boys in his class sign his name on it and write "52" by his autograph. In that way, each student reinforced the class goal of 52. The total Sunday School set a goal of 1,225. Posters were put on walls, bulletin boards, and doors. Every poster announced the goal of 1,225, but each differently—in German, Spanish, Greek, upper and lower case letters, Gothic and Roman numerals.

STEP 117   Advertise Attendance Goals
Advertise your attendance goals. This will help people identify with the goal and will build excitement and enthusiasm as the class works together to reach the goal. Unless everyone accepts the goal, it will not achieve its objective. Remember, goals must be bought and owned or the goal will not motivate class members to work for growth.

11

HOW TO SET AN ATTENDANCE GOAL

STEP 118   Set Reachable Goals
In setting your goals, be sure to set reachable goals. Goals that are unreachable discourage people and kill momentum. A missed goal is like a broken bone in the body—it takes a long time to heal. When you set an unreachable goal and fail to reach it, class members will be reluctant to support a reachable goal the next time.

SMART GOALS
Specific Goals
Measurable Goals
Attainable Goals
Reachable Goals
Time Table Goals

Do not set Friend Day output goals. Set an input goal for each to enroll a friend and bring a friend. A Free Methodist church in Michigan of approximately 100 in attendance, set an output goal of 200. There were 194 in attendance, the largest attendance in the history of the church. Because they missed their goal of 200 they were discouraged, when there should have been the greatest excitement because they had reached their highest attendance ever.

STEP 119 Know the Strengths and Weaknesses of Your Class

Know the strengths and weaknesses of your class before setting your goals. If your class members have a wide circle of friends outside the church, you will have a larger prospect base with which to work. Conversely, if the class is inbred with few contacts outside the class, it will be more difficult to find the needed prospects.

Sometimes the class has problems and it is not the time to reach out. If there is someone with a death or crisis, the members are preoccupied with the problem and are not mentally ready to reach out in growth. Knowing your strengths will help you feel the pulse of your class.

Also, if the church corporately has gone through a split, financial crisis, leadership problem, or other major setback, it should evaluate carefully when would be the best time for an outreach campaign. Just as there are times when the sick need to go to bed to recuperate, so there is a time for church inreach, not outreach.

STEP 120 Set Goals Based on Past Records

Examine past statistics to determine the best time to plan your outreach day, the day you want class members to bring their (F. R. A. N. s) friends, relatives, associates, and neighbors to the class. Generally, the biggest attended Sunday in the fall of the year tends to be the last Sunday in October (time change Sunday). The largest attended day in the spring traditionally is Easter. The second largest attended Sunday in the spring is Mother's Day.

Choose a day that does not have built-in barriers to the unchurched. Don't plan Sunday School outreach for Labor Day weekend or during the Fourth of July holiday when there is a natural dip in the attendance. The minister who tried to have his largest attendance on Labor Day weekend, or the Sunday after Easter, claiming, "Anybody can get a crowd on Easter; I want to build an attendance to show our people love God," had missed the whole purpose of an attendance campaign. A high attendance should do more than demonstrate the loyalty of the faithful. It should reach visitors (pre-evangelism), electrify everyone when the attendance is doubled, and bring men, women, and children to a saving faith in Jesus Christ. So plan for Sunday School growth when the best results are possible. Then you will be a good steward of your time, energy, and money. Therefore, plan to grow on those days when there are the fewest attendance barriers and the unchurched are most likely to attend.

If you are planning a campaign for several Sundays, plan a high attendance on the last Sunday of your campaign. Some criticize this, saying that it only gets a crowd and makes small class teaching impossible. However, the "high day" is only a return to the old-fashioned rally day, where all pupils assembled in the auditorium to "rally" enthusiasm for Sunday School. Most teachers need to break lethargy and infuse the pupils with expectation. A "double day" convinces the pupils it can be done again and again, until the class is permanently doubled.

STEP 121 Pray for Wisdom in Goal-Setting
Pray for God's guidance in setting your goals. Set a goal to do what you believe God wants you to do. Long before you set an attendance goal or choose an outreach campaign, add the item to your prayer list. (1) Ask God to give you wisdom in setting goals and campaigns. (2) Pray over them until you feel comfortable about the goal or campaign. (3) Consider the problems and barriers before publicly announcing the task. (4) When you finally make a decision by prayer, then get off your knees to make it work out in reality.

STEP 122 Set Goals by Faith'
The one unique feature of the church leaders of growing

churches around the world is that they are people of faith. There are three steps to using faith to move mountains (Mark 11:22-23) or to get things from God. I believe faith is the key to building a Sunday School class or revitalizing a church. First, the leader must be living by faith (Rom. 1:17). This is called the faith experience. Second, the leader must make a faith expression. Since Christianity is confessional in the initial expression of salvation (10:9) and we are daily to confess our faith by our lives, then it is only natural that God expects us to express our faith in Christian service. Therefore, by faith you should set a "faith goal" for your Sunday School class. Jesus commanded we should say in faith what we desire, "For assuredly, I say to you, whoever says to this mountain, 'Be removed and be cast into the sea,' and does not doubt in his heart, but believes that those things he says will come to pass, he will have whatever he says" (Mark 11:23). This leads to the third step which is a faith event. Just as a church plans an evangelistic endeavor by faith to reach people with the Gospel (revival meeting, literature distribution, youth rally, etc.), just so leaders can plan a Sunday School Outreach Campaign (Friend Day) which is a corporate expression of faith. When a person is converted, it is the result of the faith of the leadership and the followers.

STEP 123   Look for Confirmation in Scripture
Make sure your goals are biblical, that is, they fit the principles of the Bible. Proof texting is not enough; goals should grow out of Bible study and be in harmony with the Scriptures. This is always a good procedure when attempting to discern the will of God.

STEP 124   Know the Law of the Two-Humped Camel
When we describe the way a Sunday School grows over the course of a year, we speak of the "law of the two-humped camel." A growing Sunday School will have an attendance chart that looks like a two-humped camel. Growth is experienced in the spring and fall; attendance dips in the summer and winter (unless the area is impacted by holiday, vacation, etc.). Since

we know when Sunday Schools grow, set attendance goals in the growth seasons, not at other times of the year.

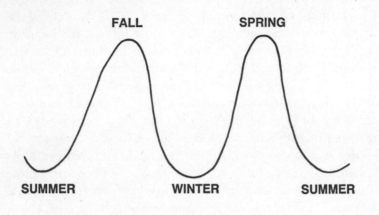

There are 36 to 37 weeks in the Sunday School growth year (the Sunday after Labor Day until the Sunday before Memorial Day weekend). Plan growth in the fall and spring, the primary growth weeks in the Sunday School.

STEP 125 Plan a Fall and Spring Attendance Campaign
Plan a campaign in the spring and fall when the people are organized for evangelistic outreach. This is a concerted thrust to bring in visitors during the time of year when they are most likely to visit church. Just as there is a time of year to plant and a season for harvest, so Sunday School leaders should recognize the harvest seasons in the Sunday School planning calendar. Just as a wise farmer must exercise natural faith to purchase seed, plow the ground, plant and water, so the Sunday School leader must use faith to apply God's laws of growth to the Sunday School year to reap the greatest harvest.

A Sunday School campaign should mobilize the entire energies of the workers to reach the lost, revitalize the Sunday

School, and expand attendance. A Sunday School campaign should have the following characteristics: (1) the lesson content should tie to the theme, (2) the theme should motivate for outreach, (3) the theme should be expressed in a pithy saying, (4) there should be a logo to visualize the campaign, (5) the campaign should be short enough to sustain interest, but long enough to generate enthusiasm and momentum, and (6) the people should reach out to their F.R.A.N.s and network them to Christ and the church.

There is a difference in campaigns and contests. A contest adds (1) prizes to the winners, or "goats" to the losers, (2) competition among groups or classes, and/or things to motivate attendance such as kites on kite day, a special guest that attracts attendance, or any other external stimuli.

Some churches are offended with contests and would not use prizes or any form of external stimuli to get a greater attendance. But, these churches could use a campaign. A campaign involves internal motivation and involves every member in an evangelistic outreach to the lost and unchurched.

Some successful Sunday School contest/campaigns have been built around the following themes:

Election Campaign. A strategic time for an election campaign contest is during a political campaign period, when attention is focused on campaigning. The ground rules are based on election procedures:

(1) Smaller departments or classes are divided into two "parties" such as the Amen and Hallelujah parties, and larger departments into four groups, each with a name.

(2) Each party selects a candidate, to be elected as class president.

(3) Each party selects a secretary, to keep records.

(4) Points are earned for the candidate as follows: each person present, 100; each visitor, 150; and each absentee, -100.

Party members get full credit for bringing visitors to any department of the Sunday School, however, new members get full credit only for joining the sponsoring class.

An Everybody-Can-Win Contest. Motivation determines priorities—even of Sunday School boys and girls. Not all can be expected to visit an "I Love Jesus" Sunday, and abandon all other projects for Him, particularly without parental push. So teachers turn to extrinsic (not inherent) motivation in various forms:

(1) Periodic prizes for each pupil who maintains a specified attendance level for a month. (This may take the form of an award for attendance three out of four Sundays, or perfect attendance may be the standard.)

(2) An award or gift for the pupil with perfect attendance for three months, six months, or a year. Graded in value, each lesser prize must be attained before the grand prize for the year can be received.

Does it work? Teachers who have tried attendance recognition have, for the most part, praised the results. Boys and girls from indifferent homes come of their own volition—sometimes with uncombed hair and unwashed faces, sometimes having gotten their own breakfast, but they are there, hearing the Word of God. As with adults, some boys and girls are not motivated as much by the monetary value of a gift as by recognition for having had perfect attendance.

Of course, a child's presence in a classroom does not guarantee that the teaching will penetrate the heart. And an attendance habit built on the desire for objects may be broken when objects no longer are given. The time to reach the heart and soul is the Sunday that the pupil is sitting in the class, eyes upturned, measuring both teacher and lesson against his home values. Which wins?

March to Sunday School in March. Many individual Sunday Schools and denominations have annually used the "marching" theme to get people to march to Sunday School. Therefore, the campaign is usually well received and acted on. To encourage participation, pastors or educational directors may:

(1) Offer a small award or gift to each member who brings a visitor, and to each visitor who comes.

(2) Offer a small gift to each one who attends on a given Sunday. One church did this, with an unexpected aftereffect. Each person present on the first Sunday of March was given a

Bible bookmark with the name of the church and pastor. The only way they could get one was to be there. Many members put them in their Bibles, and one choir member in particular is now glad she did. Ten months after the contest, her Bible—cherished for its long years of use—was stolen from her locked car. The thief decided he could not battle the accusing Book, so dropped it by the roadside. An honest man found it, called the telephone number of the pastor named on the bookmark, and the lady was reunited with her Bible—all because she went to Sunday School on the first Sunday in March.

(3) Sponsor a parade the Saturday before the first Sunday, featuring appropriate signs of invitation.

(4) Sponsor a churchwide visitation with all classes represented, to meet on the Saturday before the first Sunday, "marching" house to house with invitational handouts.

Fall Roundup. On a poster for each department in Sunday School draw cattle for each member of every class, with names affixed. In the center of the poster, draw a rider on a horse, representing the teacher. As each pupil is signed up, his picture is pasted over the drawing. When all members have signed, the roundup is completed. At the end of the campaign, a picnic may include a pony and wagon for rides for all the children.

In addition to the contest ideas, there are several companies which produce Sunday School attendance campaign kits.

The author has developed several Sunday School campaigns (not contests) published by Church Growth Institute, P.O. Box 4404, Lynchburg, Virginia 24502, including *FRIEND DAY*, *F.R.A.N.TASTIC DAYS*, and *OUTREACH TWELVE*. I developed *OUTREACH TWELVE* while Sunday School superintendent at Thomas Road Baptist Church, Lynchburg, Virginia. During the campaign, attendance jumped from an average of 4,300 to an average of 6,100 in the spring of 1972. The church never averaged in the 5,000s but used this evangelistic tool to jump from the 4,000s into the 6,000s.

STEP 126 Go Forward from Victory to Victory

It is important for leaders to breed a "success mentality" in

154 Steps to Revitalize Your Sunday School

workers. If they get discouraged or become despondent over failure, it's hard for God to use them. So leaders must keep them (1) faith-oriented, (2) future-oriented, and (3) victory-oriented. Plan small victories (input goals) so they can build up their confidence to reach for higher goals.

Remember, the church goes forward from faith to faith (Rom. 1:17), from grace to grace (John 1:16) and from victory to victory. There must be progress, just as there must be growth, so there must be a victory. As your Sunday School reaches a goal, remind the workers of the victory. This will motivate them to strive for greater goals in the future.

STEP 127 Recognize the Clenched Fist

Remember the "Law of the Clenched Fist." This principle is built on the law that pressure builds the body. That's why runners put pressure on their legs and lungs, to strengthen their bodies for the race. Weight lifters do the same thing. They pump iron, i.e., put pressure on their bodies to build them up.

PRESSURE BUILDS THE BODY OF CHRIST
1 Vision of reaching people puts pressure on church members.
2 A goal of placing a Bible in every home in the area is pressure.
3 A Sunday School campaign puts pressure on all to be included.

Growing Sunday Schools should plan no more than two attendance campaigns per year, one each in the spring and fall. Then the campaigns should not be longer than six or seven weeks as people get tired of them. If you have too many campaigns, the people will not work as hard as they can during the next campaign to find prospects, excite students, phone, write, and visit. Relax the attendance drive during the Christmas holidays, the snows of January, and again during the summer.

STEP 128 Be Careful of Over-Exercise

A man can keep his fist taut only so long, then the muscles give out. Likewise, a Sunday School leader can put pressure on his workers for only a short time. Just as a runner who puts too much pressure on his body causes a stroke, too much pressure on the body of Christ builds up resentment or resignation in workers.

Too much exercise can lead to a heart attack or stroke in the physical body. In the spiritual body, it can lead to discouragement or other more serious problems which become counterproductive in the cause of Christ.

STEP 129 Follow the Law of Creek Jumping

Remember, the "Law of Creek Jumping" states the wider the creek, the faster you have to run to clear it. Getting a running start before jumping a creek is illustrative of building up momentum or credibility before an attendance campaign. In Sunday School, the larger the goal, the longer it takes to convince workers they can reach it. It's not that you must convince yourself, you must build up confidence in others. A church leader must build "believability" in the program and the church's ability to reach a goal.

Plan a six- or seven-week spring or fall campaign with the high Sunday as the last day. Don't read this book and plan to double your class next week. Pray to double, plan to double, and promote to double. But remember this: A teacher can't lead if his class won't follow, and pupils won't work to double their class unless their teacher takes the time to convince them it can be done.

STEP 130 Do Not Attempt High Goals on Short Notice

The obvious application of the law of creek jumping is not to attempt high goals before the people have a basis to trust the new program or believe in your leadership.

STEP 131 Input Goals Build Credibility in a Campaign

One way to build both momentum and credibility as you prepare to build your class is by first achieving input goals. This will help your class believe God for bigger goals. Any class can set a goal to gather prospects, send out postcards, make phone calls, etc. This *faith experience* leads to the *faith expression* that leads to the *faith event* (see step 122).

STEP 132   Gather Twice the Number of Prospects

The first input goal you will want to achieve is finding prospects or receptive-responsive people you can reach in the campaign. Therefore, at the beginning of an attendance campaign, attempt to gather at least twice as many prospects as there are in attendance.

Some will promise to attend but find an excuse not to be present. Some of the regulars will choose not to attend on a special outreach day. Therefore, begin with twice the prospects before the campaign begins.

HOW TO FIND PROSPECTS

STEP 133   Search Records for Prospects

Prospects are the gold of growth. Someone has suggested the new "golden rule" is, "He that hath the gold makes the rules." It might be stated by way of application to Sunday School growth, "He that hath the prospects [gold] hath the growth." Just as a prospector will expend great amounts of energy looking for a vein of gold to mine, so we ought to look for prospects, our gold of growth.

One place to find prospects is to check your Sunday School records. Former members who have dropped out of Sunday School can be reclaimed for Christ, but only if you know who they are. Also, anyone who has visited the class in the past six months is a prospect who should be pursued.

STEP 134   Conduct a Buddy Hunt for Prospects

Another way to find prospects is to conduct a "Buddy Hunt." Ask class members for the names of friends, relatives, associates, and neighbors who could be reached for the class.

I visited a junior class in Sheats Memorial Baptist Church, Lexington, North Carolina when Richard Johnson, a teacher, was conducting a buddy hunt. A goal of 56 in attendance on the following Easter was announced. The teacher had kept his hands behind him during the opening of the class. I had not noticed because it is a mannerism of some teachers to clasp their hands behind their back as they teach. Then he surprised me and the class, by showing us a beautiful 56 painted on the back of his hands.

"Would you like a 56 on your hands?" he asked.

All the pupils eagerly raised their hands. The teacher pointed out a visiting lady who painted clown faces and did makeup at a neighborhood theater. The boys were ecstatic.

"Can I get it painted on my cheeks?" one pupil asked.

"You can get a 56 painted anywhere, if you'll give me the names, addresses, and phone numbers of your buddies—then promise to help me get them here." There were phone books and a city guide to help locate the information.

After Sunday School, the teacher ran up to me in the parking lot with 127 cards in his hand. "We'll have more than 56!" he exclaimed, waving a fistful of prospect cards in the air. Later he wrote to tell me he had 82 in attendance.

STEP 135　Conduct a Survey at Church for Prospects
You may also want to conduct a survey in the church foyer on Sunday, asking people in the church to suggest prospects for your class. Someone in another class may have a friend, relative, associate, or neighbor who might fit into your class. Use the following approach, "I'd like to help you win your friends to Christ." Then promise to help get them in Sunday School.

HOW TO CONTACT PROSPECTS

STEP 136　Phone Prospects
Phone every prospect. During your spring and fall campaigns, phone every prospect on your list every week. If you have a large prospect list, you will want to enlist other class members

to help with the phoning. Extend to each a friendly welcome, giving the time, place, and lesson topic. Obviously if a prospect asks you not to phone again, take him off the list.

STEP 137   Visit Prospects

Visit every prospect. Visitation puts the GO in the Gospel, carrying the message to every person. After you have phoned every prospect, a visit to his home will convince him of your love. In fact, visit every prospect every week during your attendance campaign.

STEP 138   Mail to Prospects

Send mail to every prospect. During your campaign, mail every prospect a postcard or letter inviting him to Sunday School. A housewife can write personal notes to 30 prospective students in two hours. First-class letters to 30 prospects cost little and eternal benefits will result.

For example, one Sunday several junior boys gathered in the back of a Sunday School room at Calvary Baptist Church, Ypsilanti, Michigan to examine a folded piece of paper from the pocket of a nine-year-old boy. The superintendent, expecting trouble, went back to spy out the scene. He found the ringleader showing his buddies a postcard he had received from his Sunday School teacher.

"I thought she didn't like you, the way she yells," one of the boys said.

During the pastor's invitation that morning, the teacher walked down the aisle with the boy who said, "I was saved at the end of my Sunday School class this morning." He still had his folded postcard in his pocket.

IDEAS/TECHNIQUES TO CONTACT PROSPECTS

STEP 139   Send Class Newsletters to Prospects

Send your class newsletter to every prospect during the spring and fall campaigns or before a promotional Sunday. Obviously the purpose of a class newsletter is for class communication or to enhance class loyalty. But the benefits to members also extend to reach the unchurched.

STEP 140 Have a Picture-Taking Day

Many churches have reached out to their prospects through a "Picture-Taking Sunday." This will get the prospect to your class to attend Sunday School at least twice. The first Sunday will be to get their picture taken with their buddy on picture-taking Sunday. A teacher could use her camera to take a photo of each pupil and his buddy. Then get them developed at a place that gives two prints for the price of one. The pupil and his friend must return the following week to get a photo. Then have the students autograph the picture and sign their favorite Bible verse to network them to the class. Finally suggest they take them home and pin them on their mirrors to pray for one another.

The Memorial Baptist Church in Gettysburg, Pennsylvania sponsored a picture-taking Sunday, not only taking pictures of pupils and their friends, but also a picture was taken of each class, and a picture was taken of the entire Sunday School in front of the building next to the church sign. The campaign built loyalty to the church and identification of the people with their friends.

STEP 141 Use Awards to Reinforce Proper Motives

Awards will not attract people to your church but awards will reinforce an exciting Sunday School class. The pastor of one superaggressive church sums up his rules for promotions that bear fruit: (1) maintain high standards for advertising pieces, (2) follow through on what has been announced, (3) do not give awards or rewards that are not earned, (4) use prizes that cannot be gained in any other way, (5) learn the best time to give out promotional items (usually the end of the service), (6) use variety, (7) be willing to invest funds to adequately promote, (8) inspire leaders to *work* the contest, or it will not work.

STEP 142 Excitement Attracts Visitors

Awards generate excitement and excitement generates Sunday

School growth and attracts visitors. Most people do not come just to get an award. Awards are only a means to an end. The award can be used as a reinforcement for excitement, but do not depend on them to produce enthusiasm.

STEP 143 Give Awards Properly
It is not the award you give, but how you give it that really counts. It is possible to give a bookmark with great results if it is given correctly. Some churches have spent a great deal of money on prizes that have not produced results, but in fact have backfired on them. While some awards are wrong, it is usually the way they are given that is wrong.

Should churches use external rewards to motivate members in a Sunday School contest? Christian educators do not agree on that question. Working for awards appears to have a scriptural foundation. "For other foundation can no man lay than that which is laid, which is Jesus Christ. . . . If any man's work abide which he hath built thereupon, he shall receive a reward" (1 Cor. 3:11, 14, KJV). Also, churches that use awards as part of their Sunday School contests claim they (1) unify the church, (2) attract crowds, (3) get more church members working, (4) stimulate teachers, (5) emphasize evangelism, (6) reach the community, (7) encourage visitation, (8) bolster the entire church, (9) boost attendance permanently, and (10) spur church building and expansion.

But there are also weaknesses with awards. Just because no one can prove an award is not biblical (negative) does not make it acceptable (positive). The liabilities of awards are: (1) they can cheapen the Gospel, (2) they can detract from a worship service, (3) they can offend some people, (4) they can be compared to a worldly motivational technique, (5) they can motivate people to work for wrong motives, and (6) they can be costly.

A word of tolerance to the wise: don't be against every award just because you are uncomfortable with them; the next Christian may be comfortable with them and feel they are of God. Both of you are basing convictions on feelings. Don't be quick to endorse every award because it works or someone else used it. Use only that which fits the "philosophy of ministry" for your church. My position is one of tolerance. I am not for all awards, nor am I against all awards. I have seen some I felt were scriptural, and others I felt were questionable or unbiblical.

PRACTICAL SUGGESTIONS FOR AWARDS

STEP 144   Worship Is Not a Place for Awards
When giving awards, keep them out of the church services. This will prevent unnecessarily offending members of the congregation who may be opposed to the giving of awards. Also, they do not become a barrier to the unchurched. Awarding prizes during a church service in the auditorium could have the effect of turning the sanctuary into a carnival or circus tent.

STEP 145   Keep Awards in Sunday School
The best place to give your awards is in the Sunday School. When this is done, the winners are being honored before their peers. Also, as the contest was promoted through the Sunday School, it is fitting that it should conclude in the Sunday School. Seeing the awards being distributed could also motivate other class members to do more in the next campaign.

STEP 146   Remember the Dignity of the Pastor
While it may be great fun to throw a pie in the face of the pastor if a goal is met, that pastor will have to meet a spiritual need in the life of a visiting family. Just because the pastor is willing to do anything to reach people, he must not put up barriers that will make his ministry ineffective. A visiting family may hesitate seeking spiritual counsel they need if they have come to view the pastor as a clown who gets a pie in the face. Remember, the pastor should be esteemed as the man of God.

12

ADMINISTERING
A GROWING
SUNDAY SCHOOL

STEP 147   Use a Planning Calendar
For maximum effectiveness and minimum confusion, a church
should have a master calendar and annual plan for each month
of the Sunday School year. Some churches find it beneficial to
print a monthly calendar and distribute it to their workers
and/or members to insure everyone is aware of what is going on
in every program of the church. An annual planning calendar
for the Sunday School will help Sunday School leaders plan
campaigns and special emphases with maximum efficiency. For
instance, they can plan for a spring and fall attendance campaign at a time when the church is likely to grow rather than
during an off-season. As you plan your Sunday School year, fill
in a calendar similar to the one on the next page to insure you
have everything in its place and a place for everything.

The Sunday School superintendent should assemble the
teachers and workers for a planning retreat in early August.
Perhaps a Saturday retreat with breakfast and lunch away from
the homes and church may help the leaders to focus on the
coming year. An empty planning calendar should be available so
leaders can "fill in the blanks." Work out conflicts and/or over-
lapping emphases. To make sure nothing is left out, bring along
last year's calendar for reference.

ANNUAL PLANNING CALENDAR		
SEPTEMBER	OCTOBER	NOVEMBER
Teacher Recruitment	Fall Attendance Campaign	Revival Emphasis
DECEMBER	JANUARY	FEBRUARY
Christmas-Related Programming	Stewardship Month	Prophecy Conference
MARCH	APRIL	MAY
Spring Attendance Campaign		Missionary Convention
JUNE	JULY	AUGUST
Family Life Conference	Vacation Bible School	Summer Camp

STEP 148   A Teacher Report Form Produces Accountability
A teacher report form is an effective tool in improving the
quality or standard of teaching in the Sunday School. However,
do not try to use a report form every week or it will lose its
impact. The report form should be used during the spring and
fall attendance campaigns (because pressure builds the body). As
every good personnel manager knows, people do not always do
what is expected, they are more likely to do what is inspected.
But even something as effective as a teacher report form can lose
its punch and impact if used all the time. That is why it is
recommended it be used only during the attendance campaigns

to insure the highest quality of teaching at those times. Also, many teachers who get into the habit of teaching up to a higher standard during a campaign will continue to be better teachers even when the campaign is ended.

TEACHER REPORT FORM

■ Were you in class on time? (15 minutes early) ____

What time did you arrive? _____

■ How much time did you use in preparing the lesson? 1, 2, 3, 4 hours? _____

■ How many visual aids did you use in presenting the lesson?

LIST THEM: 1 _____
             2 _____
             3 _____
             4 _____
             5 _____

■ How many absentees did you contact and try to get back in church? _____

■ How many times did you present the Gospel this past week? _____

■ What results did you have in your class today? __

_____

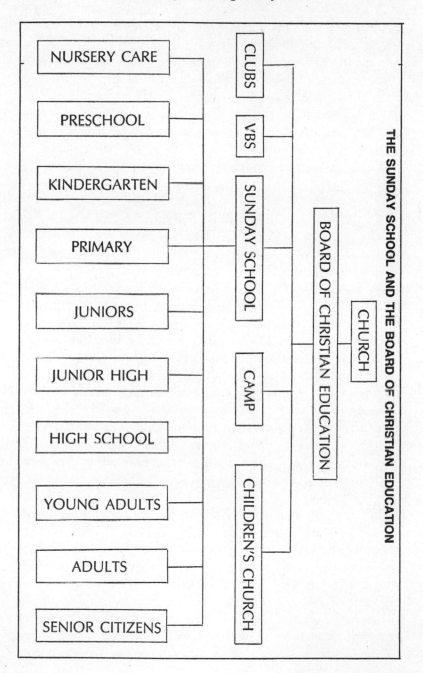

THE SUNDAY SCHOOL AND THE BOARD OF CHRISTIAN EDUCATION

CHURCH

BOARD OF CHRISTIAN EDUCATION

CLUBS

VBS

SUNDAY SCHOOL

CAMP

CHILDREN'S CHURCH

NURSERY CARE

PRESCHOOL

KINDERGARTEN

PRIMARY

JUNIORS

JUNIOR HIGH

HIGH SCHOOL

YOUNG ADULTS

ADULTS

SENIOR CITIZENS

STEP 149   *An Organizational Chart Gives Unity and Purpose*

The quality of communication could be improved and a more efficient administrative procedure developed through the creation of an organizational flowchart. The chart should be taught to all the Sunday School workers in the regular Sunday School teachers' meeting so that everyone knows to whom he is responsible and how the organization works. Also, such a chart will help to produce and maintain a good spirit of unity among the workers.

"HINTS" FOR "SUPER" SUNDAY SCHOOL SUPERINTENDENTS

STEP 150   *Add a Bell*

Every Sunday School needs a bell. When leaders add a bell or chime or buzzer to their Sunday School, they are leading it to begin and end on time. Ring the bell at 9:30 (the time every teacher needs to be in his class), 9:45 (the time the Sunday School lesson should begin), 10:45 (the time the Sunday School lesson should end), and 10:50 (the time the class should be dismissed to make their way to the morning church service). Obviously, these times will have to be adjusted if the Sunday School operates on a different time schedule. The old-fashioned bell that is rung by hand is only symbolic of its continuing effectiveness. The modern Sunday School should use an automatic timer and an electronic bell.

STEP 151   *A Teachers' Covenant Communicates Standards and Aims*

A Sunday School teachers' covenant could also be used to improve the quality of teaching in your Sunday School. The covenant could not only be used as part of the annual teachers' dedication service, it is also an excellent tool in recruiting quality teachers for your Sunday School. A Sunday School teachers' covenant communicates the standards, aims, and expectations for new workers. The following is a sample teachers' covenant.

TEACHERS' COVENANT

Recognizing the high privilege that is mine to serve my Lord through our Sunday School, and trusting in the help and guidance of the Holy Spirit, I earnestly pledge myself to this covenant.

1. I will live what I teach about separation from the world and purity of life, avoiding "every form of evil," setting an example in dress, conversation, deportment, and prayer (1 Thes. 5:22).

2. I will be faithful in attendance and make it a practice to be present at least 15 minutes early to welcome each pupil as he arrives. If at any time, through sickness or other emergency, I am unable to teach my class, I will notify my superintendent at the earliest possible moment (see 1 Cor. 4:2).

3. I will at all times manifest a deep spiritual concern for the members of my class. My first desire shall be to bring about the salvation of each pupil who does not know the Lord Jesus and to encourage the spiritual growth of every Christian (see Dan. 12:3).

4. I will carefully prepare my lessons and make each lesson session a matter of earnest prayer (see 1 Thes. 5:17).

5. I will regularly attend and urge members of my class to be present at the church services, recognizing that the church and Sunday School are inseparable. Believing in the importance of prayer, I will endeavor to maintain regular attendance at the midweek prayer service, as well as Sunday services (see Heb. 10:25).

6. I will teach according to the doctrines of our church, Christ our Saviour, Sanctifier, and coming King (see Acts 20:27).

7. I will wholeheartedly cooperate with the absentee program of our Sunday School and strive to visit the home of each pupil at least once a year (see Matt. 18:12).

8. I will heartily support the Sunday School program, attending at least 9 of the 12 monthly teachers' meetings and the training classes (see 2 Tim. 2:15).

9. I understand that my appointment as a teacher is for the

12-month period beginning the first Sunday in September. Whether my appointment is made then or later in the Sunday School year, I understand that it automatically terminates on August 31, and that decisions regarding reappointment are based on my fulfillment of this teachers' covenant (see 1 Cor. 3:9).

10. I will cheerfully abide by the decisions of my church and Sunday School, cooperating with my fellow workers in bringing our work to the highest possible degree of efficiency as one of the teaching agencies of the church (Matt. 28:19-20; John 15:16).

STEP 152 The Measure of a Good Church

Every Sunday School administrator should have a standard by which he can measure the effectiveness of the organization. Just as a thermometer reflects the health of a physical body, so a leader needs some ways to measure the health of a church body. Over the years, my research has suggested several standards by which I measure a good church.

First, the per capita income of a church often reveals much about the spiritual character of its members. Jesus reflected this standard of measurement when He said, "For where your treasure is, there your heart will be also" (Matt. 6:21). To determine a per capita income, one simply divides the total weekly offering (Sunday School, building fund, missionary offering, and regular offering) by the total number of people (including pastors, babies in nursery, ushers, etc.) attending the Sunday morning service. The per capita income for an average church is about $10.00 per attender. If the church is heavily involved in busing, that figure may be as low as $6.00 per attender. The per capita income of a healthy church runs about $12.00 per attender. Those figures are to some degree dependent on the community which the church reaches. One large church in Houston, Texas known for its millionaires has a per capita income of over $73.00.

Another measure of a good church is its annual rate of numerical growth. An annual growth rate of 7 percent represents strong consistent growth and will result in the church doubling its attendance each decade.

Third, the number of youth and adults involved in Sunday School also reveals important information about the general health of the church program. In many churches, the youth department suffers because kids are bored with the program and for the first time in their lives have the liberty to drop out. A healthy Sunday School will retain the youth when they are old enough to duck out. A healthy Sunday School will have about 12 percent of its total attendance in the youth departments and 51 percent of the total attendance will be adults.

STEP 153   Plan a Stewardship Education Program

Every church needs to plan a stewardship education program to teach their people about the important subject of stewardship. Despite the fact that one of the several titles of the Christian in the New Testament is "steward," many Christians are today confused about stewardship.

People misunderstand the meaning of stewardship because the term has been misused. Most people think stewardship is giving money, rather than managing their assets for God. One can only give what he owns. If a person realizes he does not own something in the first place, it is easy to manage it for God and give it to God. We do not own our money, possessions, or even the clothes on our back. Everything belongs to God.

If you drove a company car downtown, you would know it is not your car. You are only using it for business. That is how we should treat our possessions. God is letting us use our money for His business. A salesman must use the company car for the purpose of the business. The company usually gives the salesman instructions, rules, and limits in using its resources. Just so, a stewardship program should educate church members in the use of time, talent, and treasure for the glory of God.

Some mistakenly think that stewardship is fund-raising. They often think that a stewardship program in a local church is raising money much as the community agencies raise money. Even though money is raised for the church budget, that should never be the bottom line in the church. A stewardship program should teach church members how God wants them to spend their money. When they realize that all their money belongs to God, not just 10 percent (the tithe), they will spend their money as stewards for God. A steward is a money manager for God. When people are properly taught, they will not only give liberally to God, they will also spend their remaining funds according to God's plan. As a result, they will prosper and their church giving will continue to grow.

Stewardship is not talking people out of money. It's teaching people how to use the money they have. The most effective stewardship programs are not run from the pulpit, but through the Sunday School class. Stewardship must be taught; preaching is not enough to be effective.

Many Christians are confused and frustrated in their stewardship of financial resources because they see them primarily as personal assets that someone is trying to take away from them. When we view stewardship as management rather than ownership, the "stew" is removed from "stewardship."

STEP 154 A Total Stewardship Program Produces a Strong Church

The best way to teach stewardship in the church is usually through the annual stewardship campaign. Why a campaign? The answer is simple. If God expects His people to do something, God requires His ministers to help (or motivate) His people do it. Therefore, we organize evangelistic campaigns to help people reach the lost. In the same vein we organize Bible memory programs, Sunday School attendance campaigns, and other organized programs to help church members obey God.

Traditionally, churches have made January their stewardship month and planned to devote the month to teaching principles of stewardship to their people and subscribe their annual budget. During the month, Sunday School lessons, sermons, and testimonies are given which tie in with the stewardship campaign theme. Many such stewardship campaigns have been produced and are available to churches. The author has been involved in the development of two campaigns which have proved effective in hundreds of churches.

The first of these is called "Tithing Is Christian." This is a four-week campaign designed to teach the principles of storehouse tithing to members of the church. For one month the church is engaged in teaching and preaching tithing. The campaign includes posters to remind people to tithe. The theme is reinforced through letters and tracts. The spiritual basis for giving money to God and scriptural explanations for tithing are detailed in a student book entitled *Tithing Is Christian.*

This campaign is aimed at total saturation and education of your church. Sunday School lessons on tithing will be taught to all departments. The pastor will preach messages on stewardship. Laymen will give testimonies in the service on the blessings God has given them because they tithe. Letters will be sent to every member.

Everything is aimed toward a great climax at a stewardship banquet during the third week. The banquet is exciting and uplifting as people rejoice in the blessings of God. Faith promises received that evening and on OVER THE TOP Sunday, the final Sunday of the campaign, help subscribe the church budget. The hidden blessing of this approach is that a church determines its financial needs for the coming year, educates its people, and commits everyone according to his or her ability. Most people will give what they promise. Then the minister doesn't have to plead weekly for money. The whole church can get on with the task of soul-winning and teaching. The church offering then becomes part of the worship experience of every member.

A second stewardship campaign being used by many churches is the "God Is Able" campaign coauthored by Dr. John Maxwell. Like "Tithing Is Christian," this campaign also teaches principles of stewardship to church members during a monthlong campaign. Lessons in the "God Is Able" campaign are based on principles of local church giving (storehouse tithing is not emphasized). In addition to the usual features of a stewardship campaign, "God Is Able" includes such things as an envelope subscription Sunday, budget fair, and poster contest.

Both of the above mentioned campaigns are available as complete campaign packets from Church Growth Institute, P.O. Box 4404, Lynchburg, Virginia 24502.

CONCLUSIONS

Any church—in any place, at any time—can grow. It doesn't need this book. All it needs is the Word of God, the Spirit of God, and the blessing of God. God wants to bless and revitalize all Sunday Schools.

But many Sunday Schools are stagnant because they break the rules. This book has attempted to take Sunday Schools back to the principles that will cause them to grow—that will give them the blessing of God.

This book contains a lot of old-fashioned workable principles, because principles never change. Soul-winning, teaching, godliness, and shepherding will be blessed of God. If you follow this book you will return to the workable principles.

This book also contains some new methods. (Methods arise out of the application of eternal principles to the changing needs of man and society.) Remember, you can't use old methods (the mule and the plow) in today's economy and meet the challenge of tomorrow. This book talked about the new methods of F.R.A.N.GELISM, Friend Day, age-graded classes for adults, coffee in Sunday School, sociological strangulation, and the three danger levels of Sunday School growth.

Some say Sunday School is out of date and is passing off the scene. They only want the preaching service. If Sunday School is out of date, then so is Jesus and the New Testament. On 12 occasions Jesus is mentioned going from city to city "teaching and preaching." The New Testament church had both "teaching and preaching." If we do away with Sunday School we do away with the teaching arm of the church. Without a Bible and doctrinal foundation, our church will crumble. The future of Sunday School is as bright as the future of Bible teaching.

Until recently, I've never been willing to do away with the name Sunday School. I've always felt that if we gave up the name, we gave up our history. Yet I'm willing to give up the name in the adult department. When certain unchurched adults are invited to Sunday School, the name becomes a barrier. The unchurched think of balloons, story rugs, and children. They do not think of Bible study. Let's keep the name Sunday School for children, but invite unchurched adults to Bible study. My pastor constantly reminds me not to call it the Pastor's Sunday School Class, but the Pastor's Bible Class. I agree.

When form follows function, Sunday School will be as popular and as necessary as ever in reaching, teaching, winning, and maturing all people in Christ.

A P P E N D I C E S

APPENDIX 1

THE LAWS OF
SUNDAY SCHOOL GROWTH

People have used many gimmicks to build Sunday School attendance such as prizes, carnivals, and offering the world's largest pizza, Popsicle, or banana split. But after people have tried a promotion that usually works once, they often return to the tried and proven laws of Sunday School growth.

The laws of Sunday School growth are not new, they just seem to be new to those who have never seen them. Just as everything seems to run in cycles, the old laws have become new again, and Sunday School is returning to the basics.

When followed, these Sunday School laws have always brought results. When these laws are ignored, Sunday School results are limited and partial. These laws of growth are not man-made. They are scriptural, in that the responsibility for evangelism, growth, and maturity of the local church is on the Christian and not just on the pastor or professional worker. If a Sunday School depends on the pastor for its growth, the outreach of the Sunday School will only be as large as the outreach of the pastor. If the Sunday School depends on every member for its growth, then the outreach is unlimited.

These laws of growth reflect averages in Sunday School attendance over the years. They are proven by experience and will work in any Sunday School regardless of size, type, or clientele.

1. *Enrollment increases in proportion to workers at a ratio of 10 to 1.* Almost every Sunday School has 10 times as many students as teachers. Therefore the law necessitates at least 1 teacher for every 10 students in the Sunday School. Generally, when there is an over ratio of workers, it is because the workers are not adequately fulfilling their job as Sunday School teachers to reach, teach, win, and mature their students in the Word of God. In contrast, a church with unusual effort and hard work may lift this ratio for a while, but it is most difficult to maintain large classes for a period of more than a few months, unless there are extraneous circumstances or unusual pressure by the teacher.

There are a few large classes in our Sunday Schools that are doing the job. But they are the exception rather than the rule. The large classes are usually built around a strong personality. Total Sunday School growth usually comes from new classes, not from old large classes. The first law of Sunday School growth would imply several principles.

A. Begin new classes.

A Sunday School, by reducing its ratio of 10 to 1, will quite often grow. If the possibilities justify this expansion and if the new units work to reach their neighborhood, the class will soon be lifted to the 10 to 1 ratio, if the other laws of growth are applied. We grow by creating new units and conquering new territory.

B. Teacher training.

We cannot create new classes without having trained workers to take over the new classes. Hence, it is necessary to start teacher-training classes to provide more workers. Most Sunday Schools think that the way to grow is to first get students and then provide the teachers. This is backward. The way to grow is to recruit new teachers and send them out to enlist new students. Hence, teacher training is important to the growth of a Sunday School.

C. Class average.

The average for the entire Sunday School should be a ratio of 10 to 1. However, the individual class may vary. The average class size for preschoolers is about 5; for primaries, 7; for juniors, 9; for young people, 13. The average class enrollment for adults varies from 15 in churches with a more limited constituency to about 25 in churches with more people. Some churches have even more when there are many available adults. The average for all the Sunday School is still 10 to 1 when you add the Sunday School superintendent, the department superintendent, and other workers.

2. *The building sets the pattern for educational growth.* This law indicates the Sunday School takes the shape of the building. It is difficult to put a growing Sunday School into a small building. A Sunday School takes the shape of the building it occupies. A Sunday School that has 10 teaching centers will have difficulty growing beyond 100 in attendance (in keeping with our first rule that the enrollment increases in proportion to teachers at a ratio of 10 to 1). Growth demands new teaching centers with more space for the addition of classes.

It is difficult for a Sunday School to grow beyond the capacity of the building. There is a high correlation between the square footage, available space, and the growth of a Sunday School.

Time is needed to provide space. Extra classrooms should be on the preferred list for growth. If your church has come to the decision that it must provide more space to grow, then it is believed that one of the following plans must be adopted.

A. If your Sunday School is now constructed on a class basis, plan your space so that your Sunday School may be graded by departments.

B . If your Sunday School now has one department for each age-group, plan space for at least two departments for each age-group.

C. Then make plans to move toward a multiple department program.

3. *Sunday School units usually reach maximum growth in a few months.* Once a new class has been created, the new unit will reach an optimum limit. Then it is time, if the conditions are favorable, to create another new class. To think that a class will grow beyond the suggestions of the laws of growth, even though left over a number of years, is a false concept. Hence, the addition of new classes rather than the expansion of present classes is the way of growth.

Fruit always comes through new growth, and Sunday School enthusiasm, energy, and outreach comes from new classes. Usually these new classes win more to Christ and provide more workers. New classes produce growth in a twofold manner. First, growth comes in the total number of new students and second, there is growth potential through providing more teachers for other classes.

4. *Dividing classes by school grades provides the logical basis for adding new units.* Grading a Sunday School means arranging classes for people of the same age or nearly the same age so as to localize needs. Teaching is meeting needs. Grading by ages offers several strengths to the Sunday School. Grading helps the teacher to meet individual needs. Grading locates responsibility for each period of life. Grading locates and overcomes neglected areas. Grading simplifies the teacher's task. Grading makes the creation of needed classes easy. Grading anticipates a student's advancement in life and provides a basis for promotion. Grading breaks down social and class lines. Grading prevents a class from enlisting easy prospects and neglecting needy students. Grading recognizes natural stages of life. Grading is scriptural because it meets the individual as and where he is and attempts to lift him to where he should be. Grading makes for Sunday School growth because it puts more teachers to work for Sunday School and Christ. Grading paves the way to promote the pupil and recognizes the natural laws of growth and progress. Promotions are a necessary factor in the normal growth of a Sunday School. Students are not lost because they are ashamed to remain with those much younger. They are placed with others their age and lessons are geared to their needs.

5. *Enrollment and attendance increase in proportion to outreach.* The other laws of Sunday School growth are useless without evangelism. Soul-winning is the practical application of spiritual concern for men. In a good outreach program, there is lay-centered evangelism.

Attendance is increased in proportion to outreach. Statistics indicate that growth follows the number of contacts made with lost people. Recently, a survey indicated that when 8.6 contacts were made with each visitor, he was likely to return to the church and be "bonded" into fellowship with that church.

These Sunday School laws are built on vision, progress, and planning ahead. If you believe attendance increases in proportion to workers at the ratio of 10 to 1, then you will employ vision, plan ahead, and provide Sunday School teachers and workers. If you believe attendance increases according to the building, then you will employ vision, plan ahead, and provide space for growth. If you believe that new classes will reach optimum size in a few months, you will continue to add new classes and become progressive in organizational growth. If you will keep the students you have, reach those in your area, and teach them all effectively, you will grade them by ages. If you have the vision to believe the above laws will work, you will evangelize the lost and build a Sunday School for the glory of God.

APPENDIX 2

A ROOM DECORATION CONTEST

The idea for a Sunday School room decoration contest began when I tried to motivate a church by calling it, "The World's Dirtiest Sunday School." It was an obvious exaggeration and I thought they understood that I wanted them to prepare for visitors who came to their services. The church responded by sponsoring a special attendance day with the slogan, "Prove Towns Wrong Sunday."

When I first preached at this Maryland church, they asked me to evaluate their Sunday School. After visiting each class on Sunday morning, I met with the teachers and gave them my evaluation. I told them several positive things I had observed in their program, among them, praising their excellent Bible teaching program. Then I remarked that they were similar to a beautiful lady with a dirty face. Their facilities were dirty and several things needed repair. Old paint cans were sitting on the window sills in the Primary classroom and I'm sure no one could remember when the walls were last painted. The parking lot was full of pot holes, the shrubbery was full of weeds. The basement piano was cluttered with Sunday School supplies that had not been used in six months and the corner of the assembly room had its own collection of old chairs covered with dust. Perhaps I was just tired of seeing what is far too typical in otherwise good churches. In my report I called them "the world's dirtiest Sunday School." I exhorted them to clean up their facilities and we all laughed about it. I forgot about the incident, but they did not.

A year later I went back to preach. The carpets were clean and the building smelled fresh with new paint everywhere. Each classroom was decorated around a theme and the people were excited. A large sign greeted me entitled, "Prove Towns Wrong Sunday." The Sunday School had sponsored a clean-up Sunday. They held a contest to see which class could get their room the cleanest and best decorated. I saw a dirty, lifeless Sunday School come to life. The change defies explanation, but it happened. I have told this story all across America and many Sunday Schools have sponsored their own Sunday School decoration contest. Not only have the facilities improved, but excitement has been pumped into some dying Sunday Schools.

1. *Why you need a room decoration contest.* There are several reasons why you as a superintendent should lead your Sunday School to have a room decoration contest.

A. To develop esprit de corps.

A room decoration contest will help the teacher build class spirit. One Sunday School teacher at Memorial Baptist Church, Gettysburg, Pennsylvania hung paper daisies from the ceiling. At the center of each daisy she had a class member glue his photo. Not only were the pupils excited, mothers and fathers came visiting the class to see their child's picture.

B. As a teaching tool.

A room decoration contest will provide an additional means of teaching Bible truth. One teacher wanted to teach his class of Junior boys biblical principles of discipleship. First, the class was given the name "The Disciples" and a large sign with that title hung over the door. The classroom was littered with paper footprints, each footprint containing a verse on the theme, "Following Jesus." The boys learned what it meant to be a follower as they thought up ideas to decorate their room. Every Sunday School class should be freshly decorated at least four times a year in connection with a new quarterly theme.

C. For promoting goals.

Recently a class at the Glen Haven Baptist Church of Decatur, Georgia was decorated with hundreds of paper tabs, the type used to identify filing folders. Each tab had the class attendance goal lettered in different colors to remind the class members of the attendance goal. In another church a Sunday School teacher had a goal of 16 visitors. To announce the goal the teacher cut out block letters "16" and hung them with thread from the ceiling. Also, large block numbers of "16" were attached to the wall.

D. Bring new life.

Most Sunday School classes need new life every once in a while. Enthusiasm exists when a new Sunday School building is completed. Over the months and years the edge of appreciation for a building is blunted. But a room decoration contest will give a change in appearance and will help restore enthusiasm concerning the facilities.

E. Promote growth.

Excitement will help your Sunday School grow. When people get excited about their church, they will begin to talk to others about it. Soon visitors will appear.

F. Testimony.

Ask yourself, "What do people think about my Sunday School when they visit?" It would be great if they left remembering the Bible lesson, good visual aids, spirited singing, enthusiastic teaching, or friendly teachers, instead of the dirty bathroom or the broken windowpane. The problem is that people become used to dirty facilities or an accumulation of junk. A room decoration contest may be an important step toward getting your people to see their facilities as others see them.

2. *Conducting the contest.* If you think a room decoration contest will help you accomplish the objectives of your Sunday School, then you should plan now to take the following steps.

A. Date.

First, decide on a date. Enthusiasm will spread through the entire Sunday School if every class is freshly decorated on the same date. Do your best to avoid making exceptions. Set a date so that teachers have three to four weeks to plan and organize their classes to help them.

B. Teachers.

Next, educate your teachers concerning the project. Share some of the reasons why they need the campaign. No doubt you can think of additional reasons applicable to your specific situation. The teachers are the key to organizing their classes. It is important that they are convinced the campaign is necessary.

C. Students.

You will want full participation in the contest. Every class member needs to be involved in preparing the class. Some classes will decorate the room together as part of a class outing. Others may divide the work into various groups, assigning one or two people to make the final arrangement of the room a day or two before the final day. Total involvement of class members is one of the things to watch for.

D. Alternatives.

You may have some classes which for one reason or another cannot decorate their rooms. This would probably be true of the auditorium Bible class or classes meeting in a gymnasium. In these situations, provide a list of alternatives that will help beautify the building. There may be gardens to plant, sidewalks to repair, kitchens to clean, etc. You know what could look better if it were cleaner in your church. If a class does not have its own room, it could be assigned space on a wall in the hall or gymnasium. There they could hang pictures, posters, or other things that relate to their theme. The Church of God in Anderson, South Carolina has many small classes meeting in large open spaces. They used a modified approach to team teaching. When it came time to decorate, each teacher decorated the room divider (4 x 8 plywood on rollers).

3. *Decorations.* The possibilities in decorating your rooms are virtually unlimited. The best decorations are the ones that the pupils plan for their rooms, rather than the teacher doing some "spring cleaning" the day before the rooms are judged.

A. Pictures.

Several classes have made use of pictures of the entire class or photos of individual class members in their decorations. In a recent contest at the Memorial Baptist Church of Gettysburg, Pennsylvania, a full-color class picture was the focal point in every classroom.

B. Mobiles.

Mobiles are particularly popular among classes of younger children. Strings can be tied from the ceiling and the mobiles can be dropped to the child's level. The mobiles can be animals, flowers, pictures, numbers, or any other creative idea. For an added effect, a fan in the corner of the room will keep the mobiles moving.

C. Door entrances.

Again, classes of small children often decorate their room by constructing a special entrance around the door. One class of four-year-olds called themselves "The Bee Hive." The room was decorated with bumblebees hanging from the ceiling. Each bee had the name of a child. The entrance to the room was shaped like a beehive. A fourth-grade boys class called themselves "The Tree House Gang" and built a tree house out of plywood. A child had to climb through the "tree house" to enter the room.

D. Wall-size posters.

The entire room can be transformed by a colorful mural poster that takes the place of what was formerly a blank wall. The Tri-City Baptist Church, Gladstone, Oregon had an artist paint life-size murals on the walls of the children's departments. The children could see Daniel in the lions' den and Jacob viewing the ladder to heaven. When planned ahead of time, a mural could serve as a visual aid for the quarter's lesson. Wall-size posters are popping up all over, especially in youth departments.

E. Logo.

When decorating a room, make sure the pupils follow a theme. Then the room will be judged by their creativity in using the theme in their decorations. The theme for decoration should reinforce the lesson theme. A theme should be expressed in a logo that deals with a biblical theme. (A logo is a pictorial representation of a motto or theme.)

4. *Judging the contest.* One of the most difficult tasks in the entire campaign will be choosing a winner. You should also recognize one or two "honorable mentions." When I am asked to judge a room decoration contest, I choose a winner by their use of the following four criteria.

A. Creativity.

How original is their theme and decorating? Has the teacher put thought into this or is it simply a rehash of what someone else did? You should encourage the teachers to be creative in preparing for the contest. The best ideas are the ones no one has had yet.

B. Personal involvement.

The prettiest room could be decorated by an interior decorator but that is not what you really want. Judge the rooms on the degree of participation by every class member. Your Sunday School pupils will only become excited about their room as they decorate it.

C. Theme.

The third question I ask myself is, "How close does this room follow a single theme?" This will help prevent the "flea market" look with a little bit of everything and a lot of nothing. One thing ought to capture your imagination in every aspect of the decorated room.

D. Quality.

At the bottom of the list is quality. I would rather see a class do a poorer job than see a single individual do a first-rate job alone, but hopefully the class can work together to do a first-rate job. Expect the best from your teachers and consider quality as you choose the best decorated room in your Sunday School.

5. *Winning the contest.* When the winner has been chosen, a simple recognition service will encourage others to follow their example. You may want to give the teacher a book to help him in his teaching or pay his expenses to an area Sunday School convention. In a smaller community, the local weekly paper may be interested in printing pictures of the winning class and carrying a story about your church. A larger church could do the same sort of thing in their church newspaper. Always, a letter of appreciation should be sent from you the superintendent to the winning teacher for the fine job he did.

APPENDIX 3

TWENTY HELPS TO MOTIVATE PUPILS

If you want to be a better Sunday School teacher, you must learn to motivate your pupils. Why? Because the success of your teaching is not just measured by what you know or how well you present the lesson; your success is measured by what they learn. Pupils mostly learn what they *want* to learn. Therefore you must make them thirsty to learn. They find answers to their questions whether or not you do a good job of teaching. But if you motivate them, learning multiplies. Remember, 90 percent of teaching is motivation.

Motivation is not yelling nor is it telling funny stories. Motivation is not begging them to pay attention. Motivation is putting salt on their tongues and showing them where to find water. So to be a good motivator, you need a proper mind-set. If you have the proper attitude, the following 20 suggestions will make you a better teacher.

1. *Tag the name.* Obviously, a good teacher will know the names of his pupils. But let's go further; you need to help pupils know one another. Have *name tag day* when every pupil is registered with a gummed label.

Play games with names. Have a child find someone who has the same name or find someone whose name begins with the same letter. Those who first raise their hands together are winners. On another occasion have the pupils find someone with the same number of letters in their names, such as John, Mary, Mark, and Ruth.

2. *Investigate their name.* You have heard the question, "What's in a name?" Find out what your pupils know about their names. "For whom were you named?" or, "What does your name mean?" These are good ways to show children you are interested in them. "Do you have a nickname?" or, "Do you like your name?" Stay away from impersonal tags such as "sweetheart," "pal," or "son." Those tags may sound cute, but they are impersonal.

3. *Mirror yourself.* Make your room reflective of your life. You ought to have a picture that is personal to you; a vase of flowers; or if you have a desk, your name plate. When you identify with your room and make it personal, the pupils will follow your lead. At the office, Dad has a picture of his family on his desk; why should you not have it in Sunday School.

4. *Create a spiritual mug book.* Ask each of the pupils to bring a picture taken in their school. Paste it in a scrapbook to remind you to pray for them, or place it on a poster on the wall. If they do not have a school picture, use your Polaroid to take a picture of each pupil. Perhaps you can bring them all

together for a group picture. If you do that go one step farther and have a print made for everyone in the class. Then ask them to take them home and place them on their mirrors so they can be reminded to pray for one another.

5. *Be a handshake and hello person.* At the beginning and end of the class, station yourself at the door to greet your pupils with a friendly "hello" and a shake of the hand. Call them by name and follow up with a sincere question— because you are interested in them. If you are interested in them, then perhaps they will get interested in Jesus Christ.

6. *Use the third person.* Those who use the *first* person are interested in "I." Those who like to use the *second* person "you" tend to talk down to their pupils. Be a "third person" teacher. Use the word *we* or *us* in speaking to your class. The phrase, "We have work to do" is better than, "You have work to do." When you say, "We are having a good time," perhaps everyone will. When you begin all of your sentences with "we" perhaps there will be unity in learning.

7. *Think rainbow.* There are a lot of other colors besides black for your pens or felt-point markers. Use red, yellow, or green to make your charts, letter your name tags, or even mark your attendance charts. Most chalk is white, but they also make chalk in blue, green, and pink. How about those verses on the wall? Use colored paper and colored felt-point pens. Even your name on the door could be in flaming colors. Remember, every fall God adds a little color to the green of summer. When we get used to fall colors, God gives sparkling clean white snow. Next, God paints everything in fresh green for the spring. God knows that our moods relate to the colors of the world about us; you can do no less in your classroom.

8. *Make taste buds your buddy.* Giving your pupils a candy mint at the beginning of class may not be the answer to a poor teacher, but for a moment your pupils will like you because their taste buds are stimulated. Now, follow through with spiritual and intellectual teaching.

9. *Be a pupil booster.* You know the phrase "band boosters," and "team boosters," now be a "student booster." Let your pupils know that you appreciate anything they can do for you. "Thank you for taking the offering, Billy," "Thank you for keeping your hands in your lap, Debbie." Anytime the children do something that you have asked, show appreciation. If you boost them they in turn will boost you.

10. *Make the telephone a tool.* According to statistics, a person can contact 11 people per hour by use of the telephone. Perhaps a quick call to a pupil will get him motivated to study a particular lesson, remind him to bring a Bible, or remind him of a special speaker. Then if you give a phone number to every pupil you call, and he calls another pupil, you could reach 22 in one hour. Whereas it might take one hour to visit in a home with one pupil, you have the potential of reaching 22 in one hour through the telephone tool.

11. *Hang out your shingle.* Some pupils do not remember the name of their Sunday School teacher, and you might not be an exception. If it is possible

that your pupils do not know your name, make sure that they cannot miss it. Place your name discreetly on the door leading to the class, but not so discreetly that people will miss it. Then inside, write your name on the chalkboard or on a permanently posted area. Then another small name plate should be on your desk. Finally to reinforce your "handle" wear a name tag. If you teach adults and you want them to call you Bob, put that on the name tag.

12. *Invest a penny.* Discussion is important but it is never automatic. If you want your pupils to discuss your lesson at home, they must discuss it in the classroom. And if you want them to discuss it in the classroom you must plan for it. Paste a penny on a card and at the top write, "A penny for your thoughts," then on the other side write the question that you would like them to discuss.

13. *Think four steps.* Pupils learn when they are involved in four steps; first, seeing; second, touching; third, talking; and fourth, hearing the lesson. Therefore, "think four steps" with every lesson. Go back to last week and check your lesson plan. Did you appeal to all four? First, was there something that they could *see* on the chalkboard, overhead projector, or the flannelboard? Then was there something for them to *touch?* Let them handle a lesson hand-out, or a questionnaire for them to fill out. A great teaching tool is the workbook, pictures, or a portion of Scripture. When God asked Moses, "What is that in your hand?" (Ex. 4:2) the Lord was using the effective teaching tools. Did your class have some place for the pupils to *talk?* They should discuss the question, apply it, explain it, or show appreciation. Even Jesus who used object lessons, lectures, and stories, allowed time for questions. There are 104 recorded questions that Jesus used in the Gospels. Finally, most teachers need to get the pupils to *hear* the lesson. Most learning is listening. But make sure they hear properly, excitedly, and repeatedly.

14. *Leave mental footprints.* Actually, footprints are something that are left behind, therefore you ought to organize your hour with the impressions that you want to leave in the pupils' minds. Since organization is the channel of thinking, your students will think with you if you are organized. Most teachers plan their lesson content but never plan their questions, experiences, or activities. Write out a well-planned lesson presentation. A written lesson plan is a teaching tool.

15. *Wear a happy smile.* Toothpaste is sold by testimonials because people buy what helps others. Therefore, if the teacher is happy, the pupils will be excited. If you look forward to next week, they will come back. Not only must you be excited, you must tell your pupils that you are and why. Next Sunday tell your class five times, "I love this Sunday School class."

16. *Let helping hands help you.* There are many small tasks that you do in the classroom that your pupils could do for you. According to their age and responsibility use your pupils to take roll, pass out paper, collect the offering, distribute material, prepare chalkboards, put figures on the flannelgraph, or paste stars on the attendance charts. Anything your pupils can do—let them.

17. *Let the eyes have it.* Pupils have a hard time ignoring teachers who look deeply in their hearts. When you are teaching, do not look at the corner of the room, nor stare off into space. Let your eyes travel from one pupil to another, and talk to them as though you are talking to only one pupil. Chances are if you are communicating effectively with one you are communicating to all.

18. *Let the walls have a voice.* The old cliché is, "The walls have ears," but also, "The walls have a mouth." So let it help you teach your lesson. Turn an entire wall into a poster. If you have an entire wall, it can be a large "highway billboard." Take 8 ½ x 11 paper and cut letters. Then arrange a verse on the wall beginning almost at the ceiling and spread out the verse from corner to corner. The memory verse will be impressed in their minds if you make it the most dominant visual aid in your room.

19. *Play a happy tune.* Bring a cassette recorder or record player to Sunday School and fill the room with music before the first pupil arrives. Make sure it is a happy Christian melody. You have created a "warm" feeling even before your lesson begins. Remember, you begin to teach when the first pupil arrives.

20. *Leave on a high note.* Many teachers do not conclude their lesson, they just stop when the bell rings. How dreary for the pupils to hear, "We'll take up the lesson here next week." Plan to leave your pupils on a high note; if they leave wanting more, they have reason to come back next week. Be ready to play a song as they leave, give them a cup of Kool-aid, or save your best story till last. Go to the door and have a personal word for each pupil as he leaves. Perhaps you might promise to tell them a secret or have a gift for each.

These 20 techniques will not work if they are substituted for thorough preparation or prayer. Also, these suggestions will not take the place of love and concern, but if you truly love your pupils you will try to make your class as interesting as possible.

ENDNOTES

Chapter 1

[1]Outline of this chapter from class notes of C. Peter Wagner, Church Growth I, Pasadena, Ca.

Chapter 4

[1]The outline of this chapter is adapted from *Your Church Can Be Healthy*, C. Peter Wagner (Nashville: Abingdon, 1979).

Chapter 5

[1]From *The Successful Sunday School and Teacher's Guidebook*, Elmer Towns (Carol Stream, Ill.: Creation House, 1975), p. 94.

Chapter 6

[1]From *How to Grow an Effective Sunday School*, Elmer Towns (Denver, Accent Books, 1980), pp. 22-23.

Chapter 8

[1]F.R.A.N.GELISM is a copyrighted and registered program. Ideas and outlines used by permission Church Growth Institute, Lynchburg, Va. 1985, 1986.

[2]*Winning the Winnable*, Elmer Towns (Lynchburg, Va.: Church Growth Institute, 1986). This is a textbook for church workers to instruct them how to implement the program in a local church.

Chapter 9

[1]Idea and artwork from class notes of C. Peter Wagner, Church Growth I, Pasadena, Ca. Used by permission.

Chapter 11

For continued study of faith see *Say-It-Faith*, Elmer Towns (Wheaton: Tyndale House, 1983). I wrote this book after a study to list and analyze the 10 largest churches in the world. I determined their growth was not from methodology but faith by their leaders. I then wrote this book to explain the power of faith in church growth.

BIBLIOGRAPHY

Anderson, Clifford V. *Count on Me!* Wheaton, Illinois: Victor Books, 1980.

Arn, Charles, Donald McGavran, and Win Arn, *Growth, a New Vision for the Sunday School.* Pasadena, California: Church Growth Press, 1980.

Beal, Will (comp.). *I'm My Own M.E.! For the Pastor without a Minister of Education.* Nashville: Convention Press, 1985.

Beal, Will (comp.). *The Minister of Education as a Minister.* Nashville: Convention Press, 1986.

Bedell, Kenneth B. *The Role of Computers in Religious Education.* Nashville: Abingdon Press, 1986.

Bowman, Locke E., Jr. *Teaching Today.* Philadelphia: Westminster Press, 1980.

Brown, Lowell E. *Sunday School Standards, a Guide for Measuring and Achieving Sunday School Success.* Ventura, California: International Center for Learning, 1980.

Conaway, John. *Teaching the Bible. How-to Methods for Every Age Level.* Elgin, Illinois: David C. Cook Publishing Company, 1982.

Cully, Iris V. *New Life for Your Sunday School.* New York: Hawthorn Books, 1976.

Daniel, Eleanor, John W. Wade, and Charles Gresham, *Introduction to Christian Education.* Cincinnati, Ohio: Standard Publishing Company, 1980.

Edge, Findley B. *The Doctrine of the Laity.* Nashville, Tennessee: Convention Press, 1985.

Evette, Ray F. (comp.). *The Ministry of Childhood Education.* Nashville: Convention Press, 1985.

Gangel, Kenneth O. *24 Ways to Improve Your Teaching.* Wheaton, Illinois: Victor Books, 1986.

Glaser, John (ed.). *Caring for the Special Child.* Kansas City, Missouri: Leaven Press, 1985.

Stewart, Ed, and Nina Fishwick. *Group Talk! A Complete Plan for Leading Adult Bible Discussion Groups.* Ventura, California: Regal Books, 1986.

Hall, Terry. *Dynamic Bible Teaching with Overhead Projectors.* Elgin, Illinois: David C. Cook Publishing Company, 1985.

Bibliography

Hanson, Grant W. *Foundations for the Teaching Church.* Valley Forge, Pennsylvania: Judson Press, 1986.

Hendricks, Howard G. *Teaching to Change Lives.* Portland, Oregon: Multnomah Press, 1987.

Hendricks, William L. *A Theology for Children.* Nashville: Broadman Press, 1980.

Huitsing, Betty, Elsiebeth McDaniel, Betty A. Riley, and Mary Tucker. *Adventures in Creative Teaching.* Wheaton, Illinois: Victor Books, 1986.

Kesler, Jay, Ron Beers, and LaVonne Neff (eds.). *Parents and Children.* Wheaton, Illinois: Victor Books, 1986.

Kiser, Wayne. *Getting More Out of Church.* Wheaton, Illinois: Victor Books, 1986.

LeFever, Marlene D. *Toward Freedom, a Teacher's Guide to Helping Teens.* Elgin, Illinois: David C. Cook Publishing Company, 1979.

Lynn, Robert W., and Elliott Wright. *The Big Little School, 200 Years of the Sunday School.* Birmingham, Alabama: Religious Education Press, 1980.

Mayes, Howard, and James Long. *Can I Help It If They Don't Learn?* Wheaton, Illinois: Victor Books, 1977.

McBride, Neal F. *Teacher! A Christlike Model for Students.* Elgin, Illinois: David C. Cook Publishing Company, 1982.

Richards, Lawrence O., and Clyde Hoeldtke. *A Theology of Church Leadership.* Grand Rapids, Michigan: Zondervan Publishing House, 1980.

Smith, Sid. *10 Super Sunday Schools in the Black Community.* Nashville: Broadman Press, 1986.

Stubblefield, Jerry M. (ed.). *A Church Ministering to Adults.* Nashville: Broadman Press, 1986.

Taulman, James E. *Encouragers: The Sunday School Worker's Counseling Ministry.* Nashville: Broadman Press, 1986.

Towns, Elmer L. *How to Grow an Effective Sunday School.* Denver, Colorado: Accent Books, 1979.

Towns, Elmer L. *The Successful Sunday School and Teacher's Guidebook.* Carol Stream, Illinois: Creation House, 1976.

Towns, Elmer L., John N. Vaughan, and David J. Seifert. *The Complete Book of Church Growth.* Wheaton, Illinois: Tyndale House Publishers, Inc., 1981.

Wagner, C. Peter, *Church Growth: The State of the Art.* ed. Win Arn and Elmer Towns, Wheaton, Illinois: Tyndale House Publishers, Inc., 1986.

Wilbert, Warren N. *Teaching Christian Adults.* Grand Rapids, Michigan: Baker Book House, 1980.

Wilhoit, Jim. *Christian Education and the Search for Meaning.* Grand Rapids, Michigan: Baker Book House, 1987.

Willey, Ray (ed.). *Working with Youth.* Wheaton, Illinois: Victor Books, 1982.

Willis, Wesley R. *Make Your Teaching Count! A Guide to Improve the Quality of Your Sunday School Teaching.* Wheaton, Illinois: Victor Books, 1985.

Zuck, Roy B., Robert E. Clark, and Joanne Brubaker. *Childhood Education in the Church.* Chicago: Moody Press, 1979.

GLOSSARY

Age-Graded Sunday School—a Sunday School with an average attendance of up to 1,000-1,200 which adds a department (40 average) for each age in the school grades and a department of adults.

Arrested Spiritual Development—when a church stops growing internally (i.e., lack of prayer, sin, lack of Bible, and no vision), it ultimately stops growing externally. Internal growth (growth in grace) becomes the foundation of numerical growth.

Base—the average weekly Sunday School attendance.

Biological Growth—numerical growth resulting from babies born to church members and added to the church.

Bus Evangelism—a method of evangelism involving the establishment of bus routes and visiting people along those routes to invite them to attend the Sunday School with a view of reaching them for Christ.

Class Sunday School—a Sunday School with an average attendance of up to 100-150 where everything is organized around individual classes, or they meet in the auditorium (one room) for opening exercises or opening worship.

Conversion Growth—numerical church growth resulting from winning lost people to Jesus Christ and bonding them to the church.

Curriculum—a course of study of the Bible and related subjects which leads to and accomplishes the Great Commission.

Departmental Sunday School—a Sunday School with an average attendance up to 250-350 in which everything is organized around the departmental structure.

Discernment—the special ability to distinguish between truth and error.

Discipling—causing those who have accepted Christ to grow to maturity in their faith so that they can reach others for Christ.

E-0 Evangelism—the evangelism of unsaved members within the church congregation.

E-1 Evangelism—the evangelism which crosses barriers related to the church building or the perception of the church in the minds of the unsaved.

E-2 Evangelism—the evangelism which crosses cultural and class barriers.

E-3 Evangelism—the evangelism which crosses linguistic barriers.

Event Evangelism—see Front Door Evangelism.

Ethnikitis—an inbred allegiance of the church to one ethnic group and its lack of adaptation or openness to other groups.

Evangelism—communicating the Gospel to people in an understandable way and motivating people to respond to Christ and become a member of His church.

Evangelist—a gifted individual whom God has given to the church to work in winning others to Christ.

Exhortation—the God-given ability to draw near to others for the purpose of helping.

Expansion Growth—growth of Christianity by planting new Sunday Schools or churches.

External Growth—numerical growth in attendance, offerings, membership, or enrollment.

Faith—the God-given ability to undertake a task for God and to sustain unwavering confidence that God will accomplish the task in spite of all obstacles.

F.R.A.N.—acrostic for Friends, Relatives, Associates, Neighbors.

Friendship Evangelism—the principle of reaching others for Christ through natural relationships—our friends, relatives, associates, and neighbors.

Front Door Evangelism—inviting people to enter through the front door of the church where they can hear the Gospel in an event and be saved.

Input Goals—steps that need to be taken to reach a goal.

Internal Growth—growth of Christians or a church in the grace and knowledge of the Lord. See also "Maturing."

Knowledge—the special God-given ability to search the Scriptures, summarize the truths discovered therein, and systematically arrange them.

Koinonia—fellowship.

Koinonitis—inbred allegiance or fellowship with itself that becomes the unique commitment of a church that tends to keep it from growing.

Leadership—influencing followers.

Learning—a change in a person's experience through educational activities that results in growth toward maturity.

Maturing—bringing a person to completion or making him well-rounded.

Media Evangelism—see "Saturation Evangelism."

Mercy—the God-given ability to express compassion or cheerful love toward people who are hurting or suffering.

Method—the application of an eternal principle to a contemporary need.

Networking—the principle of establishing and building redemptive friendships for the purposes of evangelism.

Nurture—see "Maturing."

Old Age—the church and the community become "old" so that not many people are moving in or out of the neighborhood.

Organization—putting the right person, in the right place, to do the right thing, in the right way, with the right tools, at the right time, for the right purpose.

Output Goals—the "bottom line" of expected results.

People Blindness—the inability of the church to see the spiritual, social, and community needs.

Reaching—making contact with a person and motivating him to give an honest hearing to the Gospel.

Receptive-Responsive People—prospects who are receptive to the messenger and responsive to the message of the Gospel.

Saturation Evangelism—using every available means to reach every available person at every available time.

Senility—the absence of a workable strategy for growth in a church.

Shepherding—fulfilling the threefold responsibility of (1) leading the flock, (2) feeding the flock, and (3) protecting the flock.

Side Door Evangelism—first, networking people with church members; second, networking them into the activities of the church; and third, through these relationships, networking a person to Jesus Christ.

Sociological Strangulation—the situation where the facilities (church sanctuary and classrooms) are not capable of providing for growth.

Span and Direction—a basic management principle stating one manager should never have more than seven people reporting to him.

Spiritual Gift—a special ability given by the Holy Spirit to enable Christians to do productive service in the body of Christ.

St. John's Syndrome—a characteristic of churches in transition from the first to second generation occurring as a church leaves its love for Christ as expressed in soul-winning and teaching the Word of God.

Stairstepping—a systematic and natural approach of bringing people to Christ one step at a time.

Sunday School—the reaching, teaching, winning, maturing arm of the church (cf. Deut. 31:12).

Sunday School Superintendent—the extension of the pastor's organizational and administrative responsibilities, supervising the educational program of the church.

Sunday School Teacher—the extension of pastoral ministry into the life of the class.

Superaggressive Evangelism—the attitude that the Christian should be energetic and innovative in giving the Gospel to every person.

Teaching—guiding the learning activities that meet human needs.

Teaching (gift)—the God-given ability to make the Word of God clear and to effectively apply it to lives.

Testimony Evangelism—sharing our experience in Jesus Christ with other people so that they too will want to experience what we have in Christ.

Transfer Growth—numerical church growth resulting from Christians of "like-faith and like-practice" who join a church.

WASP—White Anglo-Saxon Protestant.

White Flight—see "Ethnikitis."

Winning—communicating the Gospel in an understandable manner and motivating a person to respond.

INDEX